P9-EML-766

THE BIBLE -

The Living Word of
Revelation

THE BIBLE -
The Living Word of Revelation

Edited by Merrill C. Tenney

With Essays by:

John H. Gerstner

R. Laird Harris

Kenneth S. Kantzer

John W. Montgomery

James I. Packer

Clark H. Pinnock

Merrill C. Tenney

John F. Walvoord

Marten H. Woudstra

Edward J. Young

ZONDERVAN PUBLISHING HOUSE
Grand Rapids, Michigan

THE BIBLE — The Living Word of Revelation
Copyright © 1968 by Zondervan Publishing House,
Grand Rapids, Michigan.

All rights reserved.

No portion of this book may be reproduced in any
way without the written permission of the publisher,
except for brief excerpts in magazine reviews, etc.

An Evangelical Theological Society Publication
      Monograph No. 6.

Library of Congress Catalog Card number 69-11632

Printed in the United States of America

THE EVANGELICAL THEOLOGICAL SOCIETY
(organized 1949)

Purpose
"To foster conservative Biblical scholarship by providing a medium
for the oral exchange and written expression of thought and research in
the general field of the theological disciplines as centered in the Scriptures."

Constitution, Art. II

Doctrinal Basis
"The Bible alone, and the Bible in its entirety, is the Word of God
written, and therefore inerrant in the autographs."

220.1
T29
35568

To the Memory of
V. RAYMOND EDMAN
FRIEND OF MANY YEARS
and
Lover of the Word of God

Preface

The essays incorporated into this symposium are an attempt to present in positive and relevant fashion the reflections of ten evangelical scholars on the subject of the revealed Word of God. In an age of relativism and skepticism they declare their confidence in the divine origin and authority of the Holy Scriptures as the Word of God to men, revealed to and through His prophets and apostles. Certainty without presumptuousness, clarity without naiveté, and scholarship without pedantry have been their aim. Many other works more extensive than this volume have been written on the subject of the authenticity and inspiration of the Bible, but this book is intended to speak in modern terms while presenting historic truth.

Each of the ten authors represents a different church affiliation, and for the most part a different school and/or field of scholarship. Probably no two would accord exactly in all respects in theological or ecclesiastical beliefs. Nevertheless they agree that the written Word must be the accepted basis for their faith, however they might differ in its detailed interpretation.

Variations in style may be expected, for "the style is the man." Editorial changes have been relatively few, for the editor has sought to preserve the living voice of the individual. In a composite work of this kind absolute uniformity is impossible, but logical progress of development and integration of the main concepts have been studiously cultivated.

This book is intended for laymen and theologians alike. It is hoped that it will stimulate both to a fuller consideration of the claims of the Bible for itself, and that it will provide some fresh approaches to the fundamental question of the source of authority in Christian faith.

Acknowledgments of indebtedness are due to the Moody Bible Institute, which first published the essay on "The Word of God" in its *Founder's Week Messages of 1966*, and to the publisher of *Christianity Today* for permission to quote at length from the article by Donald R. Neiswander in the issue of November 25, 1966. The editor wishes to express his thanks to the participants who cooperated in this venture while operating under the pressure of heavy schedules, to his wife, Helen J. Tenney, who gave invaluable assistance in editing the articles, and to Miss Margaret Heindl, who transcribed them for publication.

MERRILL C. TENNEY

Wheaton, Illinois

Contents

Preface

THE MEANING OF THE WORD
Merrill C. Tenney

Merrill C. Tenney

Merrill C. Tenney is Dean of the Graduate School of Wheaton College, Wheaton, Illinois, and J. P. Williston Professor of Bible and Theology. He was Professor of New Testament in Gordon College of Theology and Missions in Boston, Massachusetts from 1930-1943, and has served at Wheaton from 1943 until the present. He is General Editor of the *Zondervan Pictorial Bible Dictionary*, and has written numerous books, including *John: The Gospel of Belief*, *Galatians: The Charter of Christian Liberty*, *Interpreting Revelation*, *New Testament Survey*, *New Testament Times*, and *The Reality of the Resurrection*. He holds the Ph.D. degree from Harvard University.

Chapter I

THE MEANING OF THE WORD

WITHIN THE LAST TWO CENTURIES, and more particularly in the last fifty years, the scientific approach to the study of the universe has become the dominant factor in an attempt to solve its riddles and to exploit its resources. By means of painstaking research new machinery has been devised to lighten human labor, new medicines have been discovered to allay pain and to cure disease, and greater advances have been achieved in the exploration of the human personality through psychology. Manufacturing, transportation, finance, education, social life, and amusements have profited materially from this methodology.

For this reason there has been a tendency to assume that all riddles can be solved and all troubles allayed by human attainment through persistence and insight. Supernatural revelation has been discounted and laid aside as belonging to an age when ignorance and credulity prevailed. Modern man believes that if only he is given the proper tools and sufficient time, he can solve every problem that vexes humanity.

Within the dimension of material existence there has been an amazing progress in knowledge. The last half-century has brought to light more information concerning the chemical and physical properties of the world than the entire preceding period of recorded history. It is estimated that ninety per cent of all known scientists are now living, and the professional journals containing their discoveries have multiplied at such a rate that no one person could possibly read them.

Notwithstanding this amazing proliferation of knowledge, there are still some important questions that remain unanswered. The structure of the universe may imply a creative Designer, but no scholar has yet succeeded in isolating and describing that Mind by scientific method. No historian has yet been able to write a complete account of His part in history, although His providential intervention in human affairs seems apparent. A careful description of the world may catalog the stars and even identify the materials from which they are made. It may determine their distance and the velocity of their motion, but it cannot explain why they were lighted and impelled into space. Neither can it inform us whether that creative Mind is friendly or hostile, forgiving or unbending, compassionate or aloof.

If man is to live intelligently and with hope, he must have an answer to these problems, nor can he afford to wait for someone to discover the answer. If personal destiny in this world and the next is contingent upon a proper relation to a sovereign God, he cannot delay his decisions until some future generation uncovers the truth concerning Him.

How can any reliable knowledge concerning God be attained? The natural world may reflect His intelligence and workmanship, but it cannot depict Him exactly, any more than the table that a craftsman constructs will give a complete picture of its maker. The mystical experiences of those who seek God are so highly subjective and so divergent that they do not afford a common representation of His person. On the contrary, they often tell more about the individuals who seek than about the One whom they profess to find.

Some degree of insight into human personality may be achieved by observing a man's habits or by the interchange of conversation. Even the keenest analysis, however, may be wrongly focused so that the evaluation of another human individual may prove to be erroneous. Motives can be misunderstood, underlying traits may seldom if ever be detected, and emotions can be masked. If men cannot by investigation penetrate the inner depths of each other, how shall they be able to understand an infinite personality?

Personality can be known only by self-disclosure. If a person does not choose to speak, his real self may never be known. If God declares His mind and purposes by some sort of communication, then He can be approached on the conditions which He has established, and He can be known adequately to the extent that He chooses to convey His message by intelligible media.

The ultimate questions of life can be answered only by the One who created it. Plato, one of the greatest philosophers of antiquity, narrates in the *Phaedo* his master Socrates' discussion of immortality with some disciples. In the course of the conversation one of them, Simmias, made the following statement: "I think a man's duty is one of two things: either to be taught or to find out where the truth is, or if he cannot, at least to take the best possible human doctrine and the hardest to disprove, and to ride on this like a raft over the waters of life and take the risk; unless he could have a more seaworthy vessel to carry him more safely and with less danger, some divine doctrine [or, as Jowett translates it, "some word of God"] to bring him through."[1]

Through these words which Plato either quoted from Simmias or else attributed to him, he expressed his conviction that only a revelation from God could supply an adequate key to the mysteries of origin, purpose, and destiny. Facts concerning the material world may be discovered, collected, classified, and interpreted with results that are reliable and beneficial to mankind. The discovery of the Salk vaccine was a boon to humanity because it arrested the plague of poliomyelitis, and so saved or prolonged the lives of many potential victims. The Salk vaccine, however, could give no assurance of purpose in life, nor explain why life should be worth living. Only the knowledge of God can provide that answer.

This knowledge of God, adapted to the conditions and dilemmas of human existence, can be found in the Bible. The opening sentence of the Epistle to the Hebrews is, "God . . . hath spoken." Upon this affirmation, qualified to allow for various methods, agencies, and stages of communication, are based the authority and content of Christian theology. Where Plato wistfully speculated, the inspired Scriptures speak with certainty.

The Biblical doctrine of the Word of God is the elaboration of this truth. The Old and New Testaments both employ the phrase to indicate that God has declared His purposes to the intelligence of man. Whether the concept be taken literally in the sense of audible speech or of visible record, or whether it be the inward impartation of the mind of God to the spirit of man, or the out-

ward acts of God in history and in the incarnation of Christ, the
Bible asserts unmistakably that He has revealed Himself through
His Word.

THE DOCTRINE OF THE WORD OF GOD IN THE OLD TESTAMENT

The initial presentation of this idea appears in Genesis. Following the opening assertion of the existence of God ("In the
beginning, God . . ." Genesis 1:1), the details of the creative
process follow. Each of them is introduced by the phrase, "And
God said. . . ." The utterance of God projected His power, and
matter came into being. The world thus created was an expression of His mind and will; in a sense, it was His word.
John's gospel asserts the same truth: "In the beginning was the
Word, and the Word was with God, and the Word was God . . .
All things were made by him; and without him was not anything
made that hath been made" (John 1:1, 3). God's self-expression
is creative, and that which He has created reflects Him.

The term "Word of God" (*deber Jahweh* in the Old Testament) has numerous connotations. The Hebrew noun *dābār*
may mean "word" in the sense of a spoken utterance, "thing,"
"matter," or "concept." As in Genesis 1:1, it may imply creative
power: "By the word of Jehovah were the heavens made, and
all the host of them by the breath of his mouth" (Psalm 33:
6). It may be synonymous with commandments: "These words
Jehovah spake unto all your assembly in the mount out of
the midst of the fire, of the cloud, and of the thick darkness,
with a great voice: and he added no more" (Deuteronomy
5:22). Authority is inherent in the Word of God, for the law
of Deuteronomy stipulated that obedience to the prophetic word
was obligatory. "I will raise them up a prophet from among
their brethren, like unto thee; and I will put my words in his
mouth . . . And it shall come to pass, that whosoever will not
hearken unto my words which he shall speak in my name, I
will require it of him" (Deuteronomy 18:18, 19).

Finality of wisdom is attributed to the Word of God by the
prophet Jeremiah: "The wise men are put to shame, they are
dismayed and taken: lo, they have rejected the word of Jehovah;
and what manner of wisdom is in them?" (Jeremiah 8:9).

Jeremiah distinguished between the wisdom of his educated contemporaries and the utterance of God which they had scorned. He argued that because of their rejection of God's truth, they possessed no genuine wisdom. God's Word must take precedence of all other norms.

This concept of the Word as communication involved also verbatim reproduction. Throughout the prophecy of Jeremiah there are numerous allusions to the Word of God which he spoke to the audiences of the court and of the street. He equated the Word of God with his own utterances: "Then spake Jeremiah unto all the princes and to all the people, saying, Jehovah sent me to prophesy against this house and against this city all the words that ye have heard. Now therefore amend your ways and your doings, and obey the voice of Jehovah your God . . ." (Jeremiah 26:12, 13).

The communication of this "word of God" could frequently if not generally be attached to a particular person and occasion. It was not a vague impressionism that might have risen from the prophet's subconscious memory or desires, but was rather a specific impartation of knowledge or of commandment. "The word of the Lord came unto" is an expression that appears about 130 times in the Old Testament. Invariably it represents a disclosure of God's mind in reference to some definite situation, whether past, present, or future. Any general principle involved emanates from or is connected with the concrete need concerning which the "word" is communicated.

An excellent example is the experience of young Samuel, who had been entrusted to the care of Eli for apprenticeship in the priesthood. Under Eli's administration ritual prevailed; the monotony of tradition was seldom broken by a new revelation. "The word of Jehovah was precious (margin *rare*) in those days; there was no frequent vision" (I Samuel 3:1). Samuel, the account says, "did not yet know Jehovah, neither was the word of Jehovah yet revealed unto him" (I Samuel 3:7).

There can be no doubt that Samuel knew about Jehovah and worshiped Him, but had not established any direct contact with Him. God spoke to him audibly, and transmitted to him the awesome message that the house of Eli would suffer drastic judgment for its sins. Samuel hesitated to relay this message to Eli, since he respected the old priest. His embarrassment is a testimony to the objective quality of the revelation, for he would scarcely have invented a warning that would have disconcerted him to deliver. The narrative states further that "Jehovah revealed himself to Samuel in Shiloh by the word of Jehovah" (I Samuel 3:21).

In every instance where this formula was used, it described an experience which can be located in space and time. Quite often it was dated in the reign of a certain king, as stated in Ezekiel: "In the fifth day of the month, which was the fifth year of king Jehoiachin's captivity, the word of Jehovah came expressly unto Ezekiel the priest, the son of Buzi, in the land of the Chaldeans by the river Chebar . . ." (Ezekiel 1:2, 3). The recurrence of these words implies that the experience of revelation was not a constant trance or continuous mystical ecstasy, nor even a psychic consciousness operative at all times, but a definite impartation of some particular truth at a given time. The recipient was fully conscious that he was receiving a direct message from God.

This experience was predicated only of prophets to whom God chose to impart special truths. The first instance of the formula is used in Genesis 15:1, 4 to describe God's covenant with Abraham:

> After these things [Abraham's encounter with the king of Sodom] the word of Jehovah came unto Abram in a vision, saying, Fear not, Abram: I am thy shield, and thy exceeding great reward . . . And, behold, the word of Jehovah came unto him, saying, This man [Eliezer of Damascus] shall not be thine heir; but he that shall come forth out of thine own bowels shall be thine heir.

The promise was crucial in the history of God's redemptive purpose, for it insured the continuity of the Messianic line through Abraham and his descendants. The development of nations from Abraham, and in particular the fulfillment of the original prediction of a Saviour for mankind (Genesis 3:15) depended on this "word of God."

The means of conveying this "word" to the recipient is not always defined. In the case of Samuel it was plainly a voice that roused the young lad from slumber and sent him to Eli under the impression that the old priest had summoned him. To Abraham "the word of Jehovah" appeared in a vision (Genesis 15:1). Balaam, who was an unwilling spokesman for Jehovah, had "a word put in his mouth" (Numbers 23:5, 16), which means that the impulse and the expression came from without. The commandments of God were given to Moses in *written* form (Exodus 31:18). Hosea was directed by God into a marital experience which supplied him with a personal understanding of the love of God for His wayward people, and which became the illustration of God's message (Hosea 1:2 ff.).

Whenever the phrase, "the word of Jehovah came . . .," appears in the Old Testament, it invariably applies to a person. Twenty-eight such persons are named in the Old Testament, and each one was classed as a prophet. Some of them, like Abraham (Genesis 15:4), and Elijah (I Kings 18:1) left no written works; the majority, however, belong to the writing prophets (cf. Joel 1:1; Micah 1:1; Isaiah 2:1).

In addition to the foregoing allusions to "the word of Jehovah," the phrase "thus saith Jehovah" occurs countless times in the prophetic literature. It is more than a homiletical cliché, for the prophet assumed divine authority for evaluating contemporary events and for predicting the future. A sharp distinction was drawn between those who pretended to speak for God and those who were motivated for preaching by His imparted Word. Hananiah, a prophet, had predicted contrary to Jeremiah that Nebuchadnezzar's power would be broken within two years of his prophecy. Jeremiah upbraided him as a lying prophet, and pronounced his doom (Jeremiah 28:12-17). Only a man to whom the Word of God was given could be a true prophet.

The relation of the imparted word to the written word is explained in the prophecy of Jeremiah. The prophet had received numerous messages from God which he had relayed to the court of Judah and to the people by various methods. On some occasions he had used object lessons, on others he had preached, and in a few instances he had argued or debated with officials and renegade prophets. In the fourth year of Jehoiakim "the word of Jehovah" ordered him to write in a scroll all the words which Jehovah had spoken against Israel and Judah (Jeremiah 36:1, 2). The scroll was destroyed by the king, but was later recopied by Baruch the scribe, who served as Jeremiah's amanuensis. The prophecies were copied verbatim by dictation, and became the basis of the written works of Jeremiah in the canonical text. Although the process by which the utterances of other prophets were transmitted is not described in equal detail, their constant reference to "the word of God" implies that they also transcribed their prophecies in the same general fashion as did Jeremiah. Through this procedure the Old Testament reproduced the Word of God.

To what extent do the history and teaching of the Old Testament transcend in importance the literature of any other contemporary Oriental nation? Can its history and teaching be regarded as finally authoritative?

The first factor differentiating the Old Testament from other literature is that it *professes* to express the Word of God. Babylonian and Canaanite literature may be similar in literary form, may duplicate some of the historical references, and may even contain religious concepts that sound like the Old Testament, but these do not claim that "the word of Jehovah came unto" any specific man. The Old Testament makes a definite claim to speak with the voice of God.

A second factor is the *continuity* of the Word of God through its pages. God spoke to men before Abraham; but the allusion to "the word of God" begins with him, and carries the declaration of God's purpose through the law of Moses, the judgeship of Samuel, the kingdoms of David and Solomon, and through the prophets to the close of the Old Testament canon. With this phrase is linked a growing and unbroken chain of revelation regulating the life of God's people, interpreting for them the circumstances in which they were involved, and focusing their attention on the Messiah to come.

The expected advent of the Messianic King is a third factor that sets the Old Testament apart from other literature. It is not a mere chronicle of the fortunes of a petty nation whose rise and fall happened to be publicized while other peoples were forgotten. Within the narratives there is a tremendous surge toward the future, an expectation that the covenant of God will be fulfilled. The nation of Israel was not an end in itself; the Jewish people were the chosen vehicle for a fuller revelation and for the execution of a divine plan. In their laws, in their history, and through their prophets God was moving toward a predetermined goal.

"The word of God" includes His acts, for they spoke for Him. At the same time, the ultimate significance of these acts would have been incomprehensible to those who witnessed them had not some authoritative explanation accompanied them. As God worked in history either to discipline His people for their sins or to deliver them from their enemies, His intentions were declared to them by the prophets. Revelation and action were thus united.

The Doctrine of the Word of God in the New Testament

The doctrine of the Word of God which occupies so large a place in the revelation of the Old Testament is amplified and diversified in the New Testament. Its various writers accepted this term, and used it to express the total message of God which was incarnate in Christ, spoken by Him and by His disciples, and then crystallized into the message of the Church.

The link between the use of the Hebrew *dābār* and the New Testament concept is best illustrated by Luke. In the first two chapters of his Gospel, in which the annunciations and the births of John the Baptist and of Jesus are recorded, the Greek *rhēma* is used in the same way as the Hebrew equivalent. Just as *dābār* may mean either *spoken word* or *thing*, an event or concept, so *rhēma* is used by Luke. When the angel announced to Mary that she would become the mother of the Saviour, he confirmed his promise by saying, "No word [*rhēma*] from God shall be void of power" (Luke 1:37). Mary responded, "Behold, the handmaid of the Lord; be it unto me according to thy word [*rhēma*]." In this context "word" referred to an authoritative declaration expressing revealed truth. Later in the same narrative the shepherds of Bethlehem, having been informed of Jesus' birth, said to each other, "Let us now go even unto Bethlehem, and see this thing [*rhēma*] that is come to pass" (Luke 2:15). The utterance is united with the event; the angelic proclamation is accepted as a fulfilled fact. The power of God was demonstrated in a tangible historical effect just as the initial utterance of God created the worlds. Luke's use of *rhēma* may indicate that he was familiar with the dual significance of the Hebrew *dābār*, and that he was deliberately following the style of the Old Testament in his writing; in fact, the statement of the angel (Luke 1:37) may be a quotation from the Septuagint of Genesis 18:14: "Shall anything [*rhēma*] be impossible with the Lord?"

The word of God is thus not only a means for conveying information, but is also a creative power that produces a positive effect. Utterance and deed are inextricably connected. Furthermore, the same phrase is used in the prophetic formula which Luke applies to the ministry of John the Baptist. After fixing the chronology of John's ministry, he says, "The word of God [*rhēma theou*] came unto John, the son of Zacharias, in the wilderness" (Luke 3:2). This formula expressed John's commission to proclaim God's truth, his authority as an agent of the divine will, and the revelatory quality of the message that he preached.

In the Johannine writings *rhēma* seems to have the meaning of *spoken* word, or uttered speech, and occurs only in the plural form. The singular form which appears in the first two chapters of Luke as an equivalent of the Old Testament usage is lacking. Nevertheless there is one link which connects this concept with the mission of Jesus. In John 3:34, the author in commenting on the teaching of Jesus says: "He whom God hath sent speaketh the words [*rhēmata*] of God; for he [God] giveth not the Spirit by measure." The words of God are conveyed by the action of the Holy Spirit, who transmits them to the incarnate Son.

The converse of this text appears in John 8:47, where the reception rather than the transmission of a divine message is explained: "He that is of God heareth the words of God: for this cause ye hear them not, because ye are not of God." Not only must there be a divine transmission of truth, but also there must be a divinely illumined reception of truth. Radio waves exist and convey voices whether anyone hears them or not; but receivers must be properly tuned, or the communication is incomplete.

A similar emphasis appears in the book of Hebrews. The writer speaks of having "tasted the good word of God, and the powers of the age to come" (Hebrews 6:5). The context describes men who had been enlightened and who had been made partakers of the Holy Spirit. The word "tasted" implies at least a casual acquaintance with the revelation and power of God, if not indeed a deeper experience. However this text be interpreted, the Word of God is a dynamic force for instructing a believer.

The First Epistle of Peter plainly identifies this Word as the message of Christ. Quoting Isaiah 40:8, Peter says: "The grass withereth, and the flower falleth; but the word of the Lord [*rhēma Kyriou*] abideth forever," and then adds, "And this is the word of good tidings which was preached unto you" (I Peter 1:24, 25). He equates the Word of God mentioned by Isaiah with the Gospel which he and his colleagues preached.

From this equation and from the other uses of *rhēma theou* in the New Testament one may rightfully conclude that through both Testaments there runs one strain of revelation. God has spoken, and His utterance has eventuated in corresponding action. This action appears in His providential guidance of the trends of history as they contribute to the fulfillment of His purpose and to the coming of the Messiah, the Servant who would speak His Word.

THE USE OF THE TERM *LOGOS*

The Jewish ancestry of the title, "Word of God," has a parallel in the Hellenic background of the term *Logos* which appears in the gospel of John and in other writings of the New Testament. In a general sense it refers to spoken or written expression of a latent thought, but in technical philosophical language it denotes the central principle of the universe, the Mind which gave rationality to all things. The concept is not entirely Greek, for the Rabbinic teachers of later Judaism used *Memra*, or "spoken word," as an alternate name for God quite independently of any Hellenistic influence. Nowhere in the New Testament does *Logos* mean "name," nor does it show any clear trace of uniformly conveying connotations derived from Greek philosophy.

The language of John's gospel is closely associated with the initial presentation of God in Genesis 1:1, 3: "In the beginning God created the heavens and the earth . . . And God said, Let there be light; and there was light." The Johannine parallel reads: "In the beginning was the Word, and the Word was with God,

and the Word was God . . . All things were made through him"
(John 1:1, 3). *Logos* is thus closely related to the Hebrew
dābār, though its emphasis is slightly different from *rhēma*.
Rhēma lays stress on the dynamic *effect* of God's self-revelation,
logos emphasizes more often its *character* or *means*.

The Johannine presentation surpasses the general use of
rhēma or even of *logos* because it is applied to Christ, the Incarnate Word. God's self-expression has been manifested in a person as well as in deed and symbol. The creative Word "became
flesh and dwelt among us, and we beheld his glory," says John
(1:14). Christ is, therefore, the Word expressed in flesh, using a
human body and human consciousness to reveal to men the nature and will of Deity. His character, His actions, and His
teachings are the overt declaration of divine truth. He claimed
this authority on numerous occasions. He dared to place Himself
on an equal plane with the revelation of the Old Testament, for
upon quoting the precepts of the moral law He said: "Ye have
heard that it was said to them of old time . . . but I say unto
you" (Matthew 5:21). He administered the forgiveness of sins,
which was solely a divine prerogative (Mark 2:5-7). He
claimed that He had given God's "word" to the disciples (John
17:14), an assertion that implied much more than verbal instruction. In Him the dynamic communication of God found a perfect vehicle through whom it could be transmitted to men.
Through Him they could hear God speaking.

In general usage "the word [*logos*] of God" means His message,
whether written or spoken. Whereas the term *rhēma* is used by
Luke in the earlier chapters of his gospel concerning the act of
God's revelation in Christ, his references to preaching in Acts use
logos. At least a dozen instances of this phrase in Acts and the
epistles confirm the conclusion that it referred specifically to a
message of divine origin, disclosing truth that could not be
known apart from revelation, and potent for the spiritual transformation of the hearer. This "word" could be preached (Acts
17:13), was regarded as standard in form (II Corinthians 4:2),
and was authoritative (I Thessalonians 2:13). Paul distinguished
sharply between the word of man and the Word of God, though
he claimed that what he preached was not his own invention,

but the message which he had received directly from God (I Thessalonians 2:13; Galatians 1:11).

Both the Old and New Testaments thus speak of a communication from God in word and deed which has been historically conveyed through His chosen messengers, culminating in the incarnation of His Son. Jesus Himself confirmed this assertion by the parable of the wicked husbandmen, in which He likened His nation to farmers who rented a vineyard, agreeing to pay their rent in a share of the crops. When harvest time came, the owner sent messengers to collect the rent. The tenants refused to pay, drove away some of the messengers, and killed others. Finally the owner sent his son, thinking that the tenants would respect him; but they killed him also, and cast him out of the vineyard (Matthew 21:33-43).

Jesus thus differentiated between Himself and the prophets; He was the son, they were the servants. In one respect, however, they were alike: both He and the prophets conveyed the message of God. The Word of God is the declaration of God's will and purpose in dealing with man which has not changed since the beginning of time. Whether it be couched in the promises to the patriarchs, in the covenants of the law, in the preaching of the prophets, in the person of Christ, or in the apostolic message, it promises the same divine authority and progresses toward the same goal.

THE WORD OF GOD IN THE SCRIPTURES

How does the Word come to men today? Jesus created a precedent. If the Word of God were manifested only by deeds left unexplained, or if it were spoken only in the past and left unrecorded, it would soon be either misunderstood or forgotten. Without God's own interpretation of His works they might have been regarded as sporadic events of singular interest, but their significance might not have been apparent to the casual observer. The exodus from Egypt might have been regarded only as the revolt of a slave population; the persistence of the Judean dynasty would have been merely an accident of political history. The written Word has declared these events to be pivotal in the total purpose of God for salvation.

The teachings of Jesus, left unwritten, would have been remembered by some people who were interested in Him or in His preaching, but probably only occasional fragments would have been quoted in the literature of antiquity, if indeed any of them would have survived. The historic deed, the spoken utterance, and the incarnate life needed inscripturation to be made permanent.

To this inscripturation the Bible bears abundant witness. Jesus Himself confirmed the written authority of the Old Testament. "For verily I say unto you, Till heaven and earth pass away, one jot or one tittle shall in no wise pass away from the law, till all things be accomplished" (Matthew 5:18). While the main point of His contention was the moral and spiritual authority of the law, His language implied that the written text was an adequate and inerrant expression of the Word of God. On another occasion, when His enemies threatened to stone Him for blasphemy because He said, "I and the Father are one" (John 10:30), He challenged them on the basis of the Old Testament Scriptures which said, "Ye are gods" (Psalm 82:6). Jesus commented that if the title "gods" was applicable to the persons for whom the Psalm was written, His opponents could not logically accuse Him of blasphemy, since He merited the title, Son of God, more than those who were addressed in the Psalm (John 10:34-36). Observe also that He called this Psalm "the word of God." He accepted it as a written declaration of the mind of God.

The continuity between the Old Testament revelation and the Incarnate Word may be demonstrated by one other instance. Luke records that Jesus, in the post-resurrection appearance to the disciples on the Emmaus road, "interpreted to them in all the scriptures the things concerning himself" (Luke 24:27). In summarizing the discourse which is not here reported fully, He said, "These are my words which I spake unto you, while I was yet with you, that all things must needs be fulfilled, which are written in the law of Moses, and the prophets, and the psalms, concerning me" (Luke 24:44). He related Himself directly to the Old Testament, and accepted it as authoritative concerning the significance of His own career. The Incarnate Word and the written Word are mutually dependent and are equally an authoritative revelation.

The writers of the New Testament were conscious that the Word of God had been manifested among men, and consequently they transmitted in words the historical acts and messages that embodied it. Luke, whose writings comprise approximately twenty-eight per cent of the New Testament, introduced his presentation of Christ and the Church by declaring his purpose of imparting full knowledge, so that his reader might know the certainty of the truth in which he had been instructed (Luke 1:1-4). By this declaration he implied that he had excluded falsity and speculation from his record; in fact, he claimed that he wrote "accurately and in order." He did not say that he wrote an exhaustive biography, but that he had adhered strictly to truth.

John likewise concluded the fourth gospel by admitting that he had selected for consideration only a few of the "signs" that Jesus performed. Most of these signs were not only narrated, but also were discussed or explained at length. His purpose was both didactic and evangelistic. "These," he said, "are written, that ye may believe that Jesus is the Christ, the Son of God; and that believing ye may have life in his name" (John 20:31). In his First Epistle John connected his teaching directly with historical experience. "That which we have heard, that which we have seen with our eyes, that which we beheld, and our hands handled, concerning the Word of life . . . that which we have seen and heard declare we unto you" (I John 1:1, 3). The Incarnate Word, historically manifested in John's experience, became the criterion and message of truth.

Paul, who had probably not known Jesus personally during the days of His flesh, was well aware of the basic facts of His life (I Corinthians 1:23-25; 15:3-11). These facts constituted the foundation of his gospel to which he alluded frequently (Romans 1:16, 2:16, 16:25; II Corinthians 4:3; II Thessalonians 2:14). He called it also "the gospel of God" (Romans 1:1; 15:16; II Corinthians 11:7; I Thessalonians 2:2, 8, 9), thereby asserting that he preached a message of divine origin and authority. He drew no distinction between the two phrases, for "my gospel" refers to its reception by personal acceptance, while "the gospel of God" emphasizes its source. Paul looked upon this gospel as an inviolable trust, a message to be transmitted faithfully and accurately. He never claimed to have invented it; it was a revelation imparted to him by God.

In similar fashion other writers spoke of their message as superhuman truth. The writer of Hebrews called the Word of God "living, powerful, and sharper than any two-edged sword" (Hebrews 4:12), and said that his readers had learned it from those who had been their first teachers and who had presumably founded the church (Hebrews 13:7). Although the direct reference may be to the Old Testament, the confidence and urgency of his appeal indicate that he was consciously perpetuating that Word in his own exhortation.

The First Epistle of Peter speaks of "the word of God, which liveth and abideth." Peter identified the "word of God" with the Gospel which had been preached to his readers, presumably by himself (I Peter 1:23-25).

The Revelation, the last book of the New Testament, is called "the Revelation of Jesus Christ, which God gave him to show unto his servants, even the things which must shortly come to pass: and he sent and signified it by his angel unto his servant John; who bare witness of the word of God, and of the testimony of Jesus Christ" (Revelation 1:1, 2). The author thus acknowledged that he did not create the visions of the book, but that he transmitted "the word of God" as it had been disclosed to him.

The cumulative testimony of these writers confirms the idea that they were consciously and purposefully proclaiming the Word of God. They were not simply writing history at random nor were they propagating personal opinions. They were responsible to God for the accurate transmission of the truth as given to them in words that the Holy Spirit taught them (I Corinthians 2:13).

THE DYNAMIC OF THE WORD OF GOD

The final proof that the inscripturated Word is divine lies in its dynamic. Peter spoke of being "begotten again, not of corruptible seed, but of incorruptible, through the word of God, which liveth and abideth" (I Peter 1:23). Throughout the first chapter of this first epistle there are numerous allusions to the transformation of his personality by the power of Christ which was channeled through the Word that brought him into new life. James uses a similar expression: "Of his own will he brought us forth by the word of truth, that we should be a kind of firstfruits of his creatures" (James 1:18). In both of these passages vital reproductive power is ascribed to the Word of God. It can create life, and transform human personality. It is the stimulus that causes conviction, the summons that calls men to repentance, the solvent that cleans the guilty heart, and the pattern for a life of holiness. Other literature may be uplifting and wise, but the inscripturated Word is revelatory and authoritative.

THE NECESSITY OF THE REVEALED WORD

James I. Packer

James I. Packer

James I. Packer is Warden of Latimer House, Oxford, England. He is the author of *Fundamentalism and the Word of God* and *God Speaks to Man: Revelation and the Bible*, and is well-known as a lecturer. He holds the D. Phil. degree from Corpus Christi College, Oxford.

Chapter II

THE NECESSITY OF THE
REVEALED WORD

By "THE REVEALED WORD" is meant Holy Scripture, and this phrase is used as a pointer to the high estimate of Holy Scripture as written revelation from God, authoritative divine teaching for all men at all times. Acceptance of this estimate marks off our position from that of much contemporary Protestantism and the present argument requires clarification of the difference.

REVELATION AND THE BIBLE: MODERN VIEWS

It is true that Protestant divines generally during the past fifty years have highlighted the themes of revelation and the Word of God; but they have commonly defined revelation in a way that excludes the thought of verbal or conceptual communication, and the Word of God in a way that opposes it to the written Scriptures. They assert that revelation is illumination but not instruction, so that, in William Temple's formula, though there are "truths of revelation" (the results of correct thinking concerning revelation) there are no "revealed truths" (statements of fact communicated by God).[1] Similarly they contend that the Word of God is either Jesus Christ Himself, or man's encounter with Jesus Christ, or an event of self-understanding in the light of Jesus Christ, while the Bible is simply a human record through which, indeed, the Word is graciously mediated but with

31

which it must not be identified. We, however, reject these polarizations. Without denying that revelation, Biblically conceived, involves illumination (Matthew 11:25; 16:17; I Corinthians 2:10; Ephesians 3:3; cf. II Corinthians 4:1-6; I John 5:20), or questioning John's identification of Jesus with the eternal personal Word of the Father (John 1:1-14; cf. I John 1:1), we hold, first, that the essence of revelation is conceptual communication, whereby God makes known His own nature, thoughts, and knowledge, and, second, that Holy Scripture may yet be called the revealed Word of God in the most proper sense, inasmuch as it is in its totality God's own utterance and message. Holy Scripture is God's witness to Himself no less than it is man's witness to Him. It is both human and divine. What it says, God says. It is simultaneously man's responsive testimony to God and God's revealed Word to men.

THE WORD OF MAN AND THE WORD OF GOD

In affirming the divine origin of Holy Scripture, we do not deny the validity of the human characterizations on which the scholars of the past century have labored so hard, and in some ways so successfully. One may freely admit that Holy Scripture is partly an interpretive record of, and partly a meditative response to, the words and deeds of God in saving history from the first Adam to the last. It is both true and faithful to recognize that both as record and as interpretation (for the two are ultimately one) it has been shaped by its writers' didactic aim, personal interests, and overall theology. Such clarifications have high value, for they afford a basis not only for exact historical exegesis, which is vital, but also for impressive *a posteriori* demonstrations of the unity of saving history on the one hand, and of Biblical theology on the other. One sometimes hears it said that by continuing to maintain the plenary divine inspiration, and hence the entire trustworthiness of the Scriptures, evangelicals are throwing away the gains of a hundred years of scientific inquiry into the Bible. This is not so. The true gains of the "critical" era lie in the field of Near Eastern background studies, through which the understanding of Biblical languages, cultural and literary forms, and religious orientations, has made enormous strides forward. We hold no brief for a docetic approach to Scripture, which bases its hermeneutic, in the manner of ancient allegorism, on an arbitrary disregard of the historical humanity of the texts. Neither can we accept the quasi-Nestorian approach to Scripture which hesitates to affirm direct identity between the instruction in divine things given by the Biblical writers and God's own instruction given through them. It is this non-identification, which all hypotheses of error in Biblical narrative and teaching presuppose, that evangelical theology is basically concerned to controvert. Evangelical Protestants, in company with both Vatican Councils and Roman Catholic Biblical scholars generally, are concerned to reject this presuppositional disfigurement of the "critical" movement in Biblical study. This rejection we advertise when we call the Bible God's revealed Word.

SOURCES OF SCEPTICISM

This is not the place to set out reasons for regarding as part of the given essence of Christianity the concept of Scripture as divine truth. We have done that elsewhere,[2] and others do it on other pages of this book. It is, however, worth noting why so many modern Protestants find this view incredible. The basic reason is not, as it is sometimes thought, the existence or problems of harmonizing the Bible both with itself and with extra-Biblical knowledge. Most of these problems were known, and more or less satisfactory solutions were offered, long before modern scepticism about the truth of Scripture arose. Why was it that at a particular point in the history of the Protestant West — between 1860 and 1890, to be exact — many thoughtful Christians came to feel that they could no longer assume the divine inspiration, truth, and authority of the Scriptures, and on this basis tackle their problems as their fathers had done? The change cannot be ascribed simply to the arrival during the period of the Graf-Wellhausen hypothesis about the Pentateuch, the prophets, and the emergence of ethical monotheism. This hypothesis, though impressive in the range of phenomena for which it purports to account, has no compelling force unless it be assumed in advance that a theory of religious evolution is likely to be the true explanation of the Old Testament, or, in other words, unless the concept of Biblical inerrancy has already become problematical. The welcome which the Graf-Wellhausen hypothesis received from the start showed that the concept of Biblical inerrancy already had become problematical. Why was this?

The answer seems to lie in the combined effect on the thought about God by three movements of intellectual apostasy in European and American culture. These movements were English Deism, which was prolonged in the continental Enlightenment and in eighteenth-century America; Kant's critical philosophy, by which all subsequent Western philosophy was marked; and the man-centered pantheistic teaching of "the father of modern theology," Friedrich Schleiermacher. Each of these, in different ways, challenged the very possibility of a "revealed Word" — that is, an inspired and infallible Bible. The deistic denial of "particular providence" made it seem impossible that God should have controlled the Biblical writers so directly as to guard them from all error. Deistic writers freely suggested that Biblical miracle-stories and doctrinal formulations sprang from faulty observation and understanding. The Kantian theory of knowledge invalidated any sort of supernatural communication from God, and Kant, ignoring the greater part of the Bible, reduced religion to "the bounds of pure reason" — that is, to ethics without dogma. Schleiermacher, accepting that there were no supernatural communications, denied all knowledge of God except that distilled from the Christian religious consciousness, and taught men to read the Bible as a testament of man's religious sensibility, rather than as a testimony from a living, speaking, personal Creator.

With attitudes bred by these theories as part of his cultural heritage, it is no wonder that modern Western man, inside as well as outside the church, finds it hard to believe that God can speak to man intelligibly in any sense at all. Still less can he admit that God could cause to be written over more than a thousand years a set of documents making a wholly faithful and trustworthy account of His revelation, all of which, whatever their human character, date and literary form, are equally to be treated as instruction from Himself. On the other hand, the possibilities that philosophers and theologians of a particular age can envisage should not be taken as the measure of what God can or cannot do. Man's Creator is not limited by man's thoughts about Him. Now that the arguments for Deism, Kantianism, and Schleiermacherian liberalism have become mere historical curiosities, it behooves us to shake off prejudices against the possibility of a "revealed Word" to which these positions formerly gave rise.

THE CRUCIAL QUESTION

The question before us is whether the revealed Word of Scripture was, and is, *necessary*. What does the question mean? Necessary for whom? and for what? Protestant divines of the sixteenth and seventeenth centuries wrote against a background of controversy with Rome, in which the claim was frequently heard that the Church without the Bible was guide enough for the faithful. They took the question to mean: Is the Bible necessary for the preservation and propagation of the Gospel, the securing and spreading of true knowledge of God? They answered this question with an emphatic "yes." By way of illustration, we cite the opening chapters of Calvin's *Institutio*, which are concerned to establish this very point.

CALVIN ON THE NEED FOR SCRIPTURE

The first of the *Institutio's* four books is entitled: "Of the knowledge of God the Creator." Having first characterized true knowledge of God as issuing in self-knowledge and practical godliness, Calvin next shows that, though "a sense of deity is indelibly engraved on the human heart" (I.iii.3) by general revelation, this sense of God is "stifled or corrupted, ignorantly or maliciously" (I.iv, title) by dull and perverse man, so that none truly grasps, let alone responds to, God's self-disclosure in the created order. This leads Calvin to a powerful chapter (I.vi) entitled: "The need of Scripture, as a guide and teacher, in coming to God as a Creator." Viewing Scripture explicitly as teaching (*doctrina*) from God, first given directly to men of Bible times and then "consigned, as it were, to public records" (I.vi.2) for the instruction of later generations, Calvin argues that without its aid we shall never know our Creator as Creator, let alone as Redeemer. We quote some of the key sentences of this chapter.

As the aged, or those whose sight is defective, when any book, however fair, is set before them, though they perceive that there is something written, are scarce able to make out two consecutive words, but, when aided by glasses, begin to read distinctly, so Scripture, gathering together the impressions of deity which, till then, lay confused in their minds, dissipates the darkness, and shows us the true God clearly. (I.vi.1)

Therefore, while it becomes man seriously to use his eyes in considering the works of God, since a place has been assigned to him in this most glorious theatre that he may be a spectator of them, his special duty is to give ear to the Word. . . . If true religion is to beam on us, our principle must be that it is necessary to begin with heavenly teaching, and that it is impossible for any man to obtain even the tiniest portion of right and sound doctrine without being a disciple of Scripture. (I.vi.2)

If we reflect how prone the human mind is to lapse into forgetfulness of God, how readily inclined to every kind of error, how bent at the same time on fashioning new and fictitious religions, it will easily be realised how necessary such a sealing of heavenly doctrine has been, to prevent it from either perishing by the neglect, vanishing away amid the errors, or being corrupted by the presumptuous audacity of men. It being thus manifest that God, foreseeing the ineffectiveness of his image imprinted on the fair form of the universe, has given the aid of his Word to all whom he has ever been pleased to instruct effectually, we too must pursue this straight path, if we aspire in earnest to a genuine contemplation of God. (I.vi.3)

The argument is that the revealed Word is necessary for the knowledge of God, because, on the one hand, God has given and appointed it for this purpose, and commands that it be used accordingly. On the other hand, sin has so darkened human minds that they cannot know God apart from the light (information plus inner illumination) that Scripture brings; or rather (to indicate Calvin's full thought) that the Holy Spirit brings light by sealing Scripture on men's hearts. It is clear that for Calvin this line of reasoning, which is developed in the *Institutio* in specific relation to knowing God as Creator, has double force when it comes to knowing Him as Redeemer through Christ, for here there is no general revelation at all. The Scriptures, which are the

literary embodiment of the historical manifestation of Christ,
are, so Calvin insists, the only fount from which knowledge of
salvation can be derived.

LATER VIEWS

Most Protestant writers of the age of orthodoxy took the same
line, affirming the necessity of Scripture explicitly, and stressing
the impossibility of true knowledge of the Gospel's being attained
or retained where the Bible was not functioning as a canon or
rule of faith.[3] Turretin (*Institutio Theologiae Elencticae*, II.ii.6)
added the point that Scripture is also necessary for the propagation of the true faith, "that it might more conveniently be spread
and transmitted, not only to the absent, but also to posterity!"

In modern times the question of the necessity of Scripture has
not received much formal discussion, but the Reformation position has been, in effect, assumed and enforced every time evangelicals have expressed their mind on the destructive tendency of
"higher critical" — that is, naturalistic — views of the Bible, or
extolled Bible reading as a vital means of grace, or demanded
and developed expository preaching, Bible schools, and Bible
conferences. A pervasive conviction of the necessity of Scripture
lies at the heart of evangelicalism, and it is no accident that
evangelicals have always been the backbone of the world's Bible
Societies, and the pioneers of Bible translation, a field in which
the work of the Wycliffe Bible Translators is only the latest in a
long series of distinguished developments. The self-conscious
Bible-centeredness of evangelical culture in all its forms during
the past three centuries is further testimony to the strength of
the evangelical conviction that Scripture, and Scripture alone, can
and must guide us in living to the praise and pleasure of God.

Nor is it only among evangelicals that this conviction is found
at the present time. The current renewed interest in the Bible and
the reappearance of Biblical theology and dogmatics in liberal
Protestant circles may be cited as proof that a sense of the necessity of Scripture is actually spreading in our time. Even more
striking is the Biblical revival in the Roman Church, which
seems now to have dispelled fully the idea that the Bible is a
Protestant book which Roman Catholics need not read. Although

by comparison with Reformation theology this new awareness
may seem for the most part not to be perfectly focused or thought
through as yet, its presence in the churches is a most hopeful
sign for the future.

THE PURPOSE OF THIS ANSWER

The purpose in this essay is to confirm the Reformation position
by further argument. Before attempting this, however, for the
sake of clarity, we must analyze the meaning of the thesis that
Scripture is *necessary* a little further than evangelical writers of
earlier times were wont to do.

THE QUESTION OF NECESSITY

First, it should be made clear what kind or kinds of necessity
are being considered. "Necessary" in this context might mean
necessary for God, or for man. Reformation theology, as we have
seen, concentrated on showing that Scripture is necessary for
man if he is to know God truly, but a further question waits to be
asked: Was, then, the giving of Scripture, and the use of it for
the Church's instruction, in any way necessary for God?

It is clear that God was under no absolute necessity to reveal
Himself savingly to sinful men. God owes sinners nothing; if He
does them good, it is an exercise of free grace on His part, the
freedom and freeness of which consist precisely in the fact that
He was not obliged to show it. One may still ask whether God's
plan of redeeming, calling, sanctifying, and perfecting a world-
wide Church through the mediation of one man, Christ Jesus,
whose universally significant ministry took place at one particular
point in the total space-time structure of world history, did not
require the giving of the Scriptures as a necessary means to
God's end. In other words, did God's plan to bring men in every
place and every age to know Jesus of Nazareth as their God and
Saviour necessarily involve the giving of written testimony to
Jesus through inspiration, just as it necessarily involved the sending of the Son from heaven to acquire the identity of Jesus
through incarnation? A further question is whether one should
distinguish degrees of accuracy and adequacy in the knowledge
of God in Christ. Should one conclude that the necessity of

Scripture will become increasingly apparent as concern rises from a general desire that men should in some degree know Christ to a specific desire that their knowledge of Him should be perfect, full in content and free from distortion and mistakes?

The Necessity of the Record

Secondly, one must be clear as to what is and to what is not in view when he speaks of the revealed Word. In the first part of this essay this phrase is used to denote the inspired Scriptures, in which the saving words and deeds of God are recorded and explained in a way that is wholly true, trustworthy, and therefore normative for faith. By way of further qualification, it is used henceforth to refer only to the Scriptures, and not to God's historical acts of revelation and redemption, as such, which the Scriptures record. It would not, however, be improper to call God's messages to the patriarchs, Moses, or to any of His people at any later time between Moses and the apostolic age, His "revealed Word." So far from this usage being improper, it is primary: had God not spoken in history to reveal His redemptive plan, and then fulfilled His words by saving action, there would be nothing for Scripture to record. But it is important to distinguish between the testimony and the events to which testimony is borne. Both are necessary to salvation, but not in the same way. God's historical messages about His saving intentions, and the redemptive events which fulfilled them, are necessary to the essence of salvation. The inspired record, however, is necessary, not for the being of salvation, but for the full and exact knowledge of it. This distinction must be kept clear; hence the deliberately restricted usage.

Is Inspiration Necessary?

If, however, belief in the supernatural inspiration of the revealed Word is, for whatever reason, discarded, and the Biblical documents are regarded as no more than human records written by good men in good faith, is knowledge of salvation then jeopardized? Do the facts of saving history then become unknowable? Does Jesus Christ then vanish in the mists of historical doubt? Watchers of the left-wing liberals of Germany and America at the end of the last century who, with their denials of scriptural inspiration denied also much of the factual and doctrinal substance of Biblical faith (such as the ontological reality of the Trinity, the uniqueness of the incarnation, the transactional atonement, the virgin birth, miracles, and physical resurrection of Jesus), were tempted to conclude that the answer to these questions was "yes." They contended that once inspiration was surrendered, then by some kind of logical necessity everything must fall. B. B. Warfield, however, among others, denied this very strongly:

> Let it not be said that . . . we found the whole Christian system upon the doctrine of plenary inspiration. . . . Were there no such thing as inspiration, Christianity would be true, and all its essential doctrines would be credibly witnessed to us in the generally trustworthy reports of the teaching of our Lord and of His authoritative agents in founding the Church,. preserved in the writings of the apostles and their first followers, and in the historical witness of the living Church. Inspiration is not the most fundamental of Christian doctrines, nor even the first thing we prove about the Scriptures . . . These we first prove authentic, historically credible, generally trustworthy, before we prove them inspired. And the proof of their authenticity, credibility, general trustworthiness would give us a firm base for Christianity prior to any knowledge on our part of their inspiration, and apart indeed from the existence of inspiration . . . The verities of our faith would remain historically proven to us — so bountiful has God been in his fostering care — even had we no Bible; and through those verities, salvation.[4]

Warfield's statement prompts two comments.

First, we could not endorse the abstract, Butlerian, anti-deistic, and basically rationalistic structure of Warfield's formal apologetics without qualifications so heavy as to change the whole character of his system. We could admit the thesis that as things are, Christian faith could in principle survive in some form, under the good hand of God, "even had we no Bible" — even, that is, if the writings that survived from the age of the inspired apostles had clearly not been themselves inspired, and had never become a canon for faith because they were not fit for this purpose (which is what Warfield seems to mean). It is likely that any initial reluctance to concede this will prove to reflect only our habitual underestimate of the evidential significance of sub-apostolic and patristic Christianity, not to mention later Christian history and experience. Indeed, Christianity did survive, after a fashion, in the Dark Ages and the mediaeval period under conditions of Biblical ignorance which created a situation not dissimilar to that which Warfield envisages. Certainly, it was right to resist the suggestion that the rejecting of plenary inspiration must mean the end of the historic Christian faith. The right-wing versions of neo-orthodoxy and Biblical theology in our own day have shown this clearly, for, whatever distortions may appear to be built into them, it can hardly be denied that the systems of Barth, Brunner, Niebuhr, Herbert, and A. M. Ramsey — to name no more — represent a recognizable recovery, in conscious opposition to liberalism, of a Christ-centered, redemption-rooted faith in the living God; yet no one of these writers holds to the plenary inspiration and inerrancy of the Bible.

Second, however, it must be stressed that to say that under certain circumstances Christianity can survive is not to say that it can survive healthily. Warfield himself in a footnote[5] points to facts which show that without the acknowledgment of Scripture as God's revealed Word, Christianity cannot survive healthily. Inspiration, he writes, is "(1) the element [of the Christian faith] which gives *detailed certitude* to the delivery of doctrine in the New Testament, and (2) the element *by which the individual Christian is brought into immediate relation to God* in the revelation of truth through the prophets and apostles" (italics ours). The point that must be grasped is that faith, viewed both as trust in the truth of God and as communion with the God of truth (and both aspects are essential), has as its primary object the speech and teaching of God, the Creator, as such. The truths of God's Son as Saviour, and of His Father as our Father, being *consequent* objects of faith, owe this status formally to the fact that God in His teaching has so set them forth. Hence, as physical life is enfeebled when proper food and drink are withheld, so faith is impoverished and our whole relation to God with it, just to the extent to which God's revealed Word — His own account of the facts and acts of faith — is unknown to us, or denied by us. The reason for this is that such ignorance or denial obstructs the covenanted work of the Holy Spirit in sealing God's truth on our hearts and eliciting response to it. God's truth, indeed, evidences itself as such through the inward illumination of the Spirit, but inadequate or mistaken notions about Holy Scripture will so clutter and prejudice our minds that its divine authentication and authority as God's truth will not be felt. Not only, therefore, is there, as Warfield argued, logical failure in a professed Christian supernaturalism which rejects a supernatural Bible, which claims to revere Christ and His apostles as teachers from God yet disregards their testimony to Scripture as itself the speech of God; but also there is spiritual failure. Some degree of definiteness and fullness of conviction, and some due exercises of spirit in dealing with God are bound to be lacking where faith in the Bible as the revealed Word of God is absent. This will be exemplified below.

The Necessity for a Scriptural Revelation

There are three lines of thought which show the necessity of the inscripturated Word if God's purpose of saving and sanctifying a world-wide church during the centuries between Christ's two comings is to be fully accomplished. First, the revealed Word of which we speak is the Bible as we have it, the sixty-six books of the canonical Old and New Testaments, composed by many authors over more than a thousand years. Second, it is precisely from the Christianity which we learn from this source that we infer the need for this source to exist to teach it. Whether any other revealed word would have been necessary for other purposes under other circumstances is not the question; we are affirming, thirdly, that the Bible was, and is, a necessary element in the Christianity we have received. We argue that it is, for the reasons that follow.

The revealed Word is necessary because of the complexity of revealed truth.

From the moment man sinned God the Creator began to show Himself a God of grace, accepting responsibility to do all that was necessary to restore, not merely individuals, but, in a real sense, the whole human race, to Himself. This restoration, being essentially a reversal of the effects of sin, necessarily involved the redeeming of sinners out of their negative status. He raised them from guilt, alienation, ignorance, and exposure to the first and second death under God's wrath, into a positive relation with Him in which they knew and enjoyed reconciliation, forgiveness, and fatherly love and care. Their restoration also involved, by equal necessity, the renewal in them of the divine image. God the Creator is rational and righteous, and His image in man consisted of a derived and dependent rationality expressed in responsive righteousness, a rational righteousness comprising both worshipful obedience to God and sacrificial service of man. It is evident that both the enjoyment of a restored status and the practice of rational righteousness presuppose knowledge of the will, works, and ways of God. It was necessary that the work of restoration should have an educational, instructional aspect. In addition to making redemptive provision for sinners, God must speak to them, not only in the imperative but also in the indicative mode, not only in directive but in didactic speech, to teach them His character, aims, standards, and proposals. He must explain to them what His purpose is both for themselves as individuals, and also for the Church, the redeemed community, and the whole cosmos, so that they may know His mind at least in principle regarding every issue and situation with which they have to deal, and in which He has to deal with them. To move us by external physical force alone, as men move sticks or stones, would not answer God's restorative purpose. Only as He addresses us directly, and works on and in us in conjunction with His message, can our activity take the form of rational, personal response to Himself. Therefore a revealed Word from God to mankind, embracing a wide range of instruction, was necessary from the start. Such a revealed Word cannot avoid being complex if it is to deal adequately with the complexity of human life, "that the man of God may be complete, furnished completely unto every good work" (II Timothy 3:17).

Furthermore, all God's instruction to sinful men had to be given correctively, in contradistinction both to their false ways and also to their distorted ideas about God and life. Sin has intellectual as well as moral effects, so that, as Calvin rightly insisted in the passages quoted earlier, we are all now dull and

perverse in spiritual matters, prone to miss the point and to mis-
understand, and very slow to see how God's truth applies to
ourselves. Sin by thus corrupting mental life has complicated it.
In place of the childlike receptiveness and simplicity in face of
God's Word which was part of His image, there is now the
fathomless complexity of self-regarding rationalization and moral
dishonesty which prompted Jeremiah to cry, "The heart is deceit-
ful above all things, and it is desperately sick: who can know it,"
and to confess that none but God can search its depths (Jeremiah
17:9 f.). It was necessary, therefore, that God should set forth
His Word in corrective application to the manifold misconceptions
and oversights of man in the realm of moral and spiritual reality.
A great deal of the Bible is in fact devoted to detecting and correcting errors; "reproof" and "correction" are specified as part of
the purpose for which Scripture was given (II Timothy 3:16).
A corrective presentation cannot help being as complex in form as
are the aberrations which it seeks to correct, as a moment's thought
about Isaiah's polemics against idolatry, or Christ's against the man-
ners and mentality of the Pharisees, or Paul's against the Galatian
and Colossian heresies, will show.

Furthermore — and this is the weightiest factor of all — the
divinely decreed way of restoration was by means of an ordered
historical process exalting the Lord Jesus Christ, the God-man,
as Saviour of God's people and reintegrator of all creation, and
bringing sinners to worship, trust and love Him as such. The
heart of the knowledge which God now seeks to impart is, as the
New Testament shows, knowledge of the risen Jesus of Nazareth
as a living person, who is to be understood in terms of thought-
modes for which the theological labels are the triunity of God, the
incarnation of the Son, the mediatorial office, and saving union
with Christ — perhaps the most complex and elusive concepts in
the whole history of human thought.

The Bible indicates that to enable men to rise to these thoughts
when Jesus came, God spent literally centuries preparing the way
by teaching the Jewish people through the instruction of priests
and prophets, through typical institutions of ministry, leadership,
and worship, and through the revealed Word of the Old Testament writings, the basic concepts that they needed for this task.
Thus the Old Testament now stands as a divine lexicon and

phrase-book for the New. The New Testament teachers themselves proclaimed Christ and the Christian economy as the fulfillment of the Old Testament, and expounded the significance of
Christ in Old Testament terms (prophet, priest, king, judge,
sacrifice, covenant, etc.). In this way the revealed Word of both
Testaments forms a single organism of revelation, the New build-
ing on the Old and the Old buttressing the New, each incomplete without the other. And, it appears true to say that, just as
the Old Testament was necessary to make possible the gigantic
intellectual achievement of the apostles in comprehending Jesus
Christ, so both Testaments together are necessary to the Church
in its equally gigantic intellectual task of grasping their message,
restating and reapplying it in terms of the cultural shifts and
mutations of each successive age.

The complexity of this message, in its full New Testament
presentation, makes it inconceivable that the Church could retain
it intact were not the revealed Word constantly at hand to be
pored over and consulted in cases of doubt and uncertainty, and
as a safeguard against forgetfulness.

We conclude, therefore, that the complexity of human life
which it covers, the variety of deviations which it seeks to correct, and the theological depths and demands of the apostolic
confession of Christ, made the provision of God's Word in writing
a necessity if God's restorative purpose was to be carried through.

*The revealed Word is necessary because the Church constantly
needs its renewing impact.*

The psalmist's statement, "Thy word hath quickened me"
(Psalm 119:50), points to the fact that the way the Spirit of God
creates, sustains, and renews our fellowship with our Creator is
by applying to us the Word of God — that is, God's message, as
His inspired messengers set it forth, whether orally or in writing.
The Old Testament use of the phrase, "the word of the Lord," for
each prophetic oracle points to the organic unity of all the
particular "words" of God, as part of a single composite manifestation of a single speaker's mind. "Each individual revelation
is not *a* word, but *the* word of Jahweh. . . . In every single revelation it is always the whole word of God that expresses itself."[6]

In the New Testament, apart from its Johannine application to the Son of God (John 1:1-14, cf. I John 1:1), the phrase, "the word of God," denotes specifically the Christian message as a whole, the many-sided good news of divine grace through Jesus Christ, as proclaimed by Jesus and His apostles. The New Testament itself, and, indeed, in a large sense the whole Bible, may properly be called "the Word of God" in this material sense, as being proclamation of the Gospel, no less than in the formal sense of having God as its source and speaker. As in the Old Testament the Word of God is said to go out into the world with power to produce its intended effect (Isaiah 55:10 f., cf. Jeremiah 1:9 f.), so in the New Testament the Word of God — that is, the Gospel — is declared to be the means whereby God searches hearts (Hebrews 4:12), creates faith (Romans 10:17, cf. John 17:20), effects new birth (James 1:18, I Peter 1:23), cleanses (John 15:3, Ephesians 5:26), sanctifies (John 17:17), gives wisdom (Colossians 3:16), builds up Christians in faith and brings them to their final heritage (Acts 20:32) — in short, saves their souls (James 1:21).

Two principles emerge. The first is that what God blesses to us is His truth, and only His truth — that is, the teaching of Scripture, as faithfully echoed and reproduced in the preaching and witness of the Church. The argument that some particular Christian point of view (Roman Catholic, Calvinist, Arminian, Pentecostal, for instance) must be true because God has demonstrably blessed people who hold it, cannot ever be conclusive, because God in mercy blesses His truth to us despite errors that may be mixed with it. But it is not the errors that He blesses — it is only with His truth that He feeds our souls.

The second principle is that God's Word, whether viewed as a whole or from the standpoint of the particular "words" that make it up (cf. Micah 2:7, Psalm 119:103, John 14:24, 15:7), has the nature of a *call* (cf. Psalm 50:1, Jeremiah 7:13). It comes as a summons to each hearer to respond to God in the light of its application to himself, and the way the Holy Spirit blesses it is precisely by causing us to understand and receive it as God's call, and to answer accordingly.

If the Church could be trusted to transmit apostolic teaching undistorted, the need for Scripture would be less. But the Church

being made up of sinners who are not yet perfectly delivered
from inbred intellectual perversity, cannot be relied on to do this.
Whenever the Church attempts to rethink its message in order,
to relate it effectively to current non-Christian movements of
thought, a spirit of intellectual worldliness operates to induce
assimilation of the Gospel to that which it should be challenging
and correcting. This occurred in connection with Gnosticism
during the apostolic age itself, as the New Testament bears
witness; again with Platonism at Alexandria through Origen, and
with Aristotelianism in the Middle Ages through Thomas Aquinas;
with Newtonian physics in the Enlightenment; with Kant's
theory of knowledge and Hegel's metaphysic of "spirit" in the
nineteenth century; and with existentialism in the twentieth.
Moreover, the temptation to revert from grace to works is constant, as witness the Judaizing movement in New Testament
times, the sacramental and juridical legalism of the patristic
period, the amalgam of merit and magic in mediaeval popular
piety, the moralism of liberal Protestants and the ecclesiastical
legalism of Roman Catholics since Trent. Always vulnerable to
these tendencies and likely to petrify in external formalism, the
Church's life presents a pattern of constant decline, reversed,
however, from time to time by fresh outpourings of the Spirit of
God. What does the Spirit do at these times? The answer can
be stated with precision. He confronts the Church afresh with
the revealed Word of God from which it has drifted, and causes
professed Christians to hear again the Biblical message of grace
as God's promise and call to themselves. This has been the real
essence of all movements of genuine reformation and revival in
the Church. Were there no revealed Word of God by which
degenerate traditional forms of faith and worship could be cor-
rected, the renewal that is constantly needed in the Church on
earth would never be possible. Thus, from this angle also the
necessity of the revealed Word appears.

*The revealed Word is necessary as the foundation for
our life of faith.*

We have already said that faith, according to the Bible, is
correlative primarily to God's Word as such, and consequently
to the various realities set forth in God's Word — chiefly, the living

God Himself, and His Son, the living Christ, and the promises of His covenant. The focal center of faith, according to the Bible, is the promise of mercy to sinners which are confirmed by Christ's mediation and shed blood. "How many soever be the promises of God, *in him is the yea*" (II Corinthians 1:20). In God's promises, thus guaranteed — promises of forgiveness, of guidance, of protection, of help, of glory — God's people are to trust. *Standing on the promises of God* is the essential exercise of faith, as appears from Romans 4, where Paul pointed to Abraham as the exemplar of justifying faith. "Abraham believed God, and it was counted unto him for righteousness" (Romans 4:3). Wherein did his faith consist? It was manifested in his tenacious, God-honoring adherence, against all reason and probability, to the divine promise that he should have an heir and a host of descendants. "Without being weakened in faith he considered his own body now as good as dead . . . and the deadness of Sarah's womb: yet, *looking unto the promise of God*, he wavered not through unbelief, but waxed strong through faith, giving glory to God, and being fully assured that what he had promised, he was able also to perform. *Wherefore it was reckoned unto him for righteousness*" (Romans 4:19 ff., italics for emphasis). Abraham's faith, the faith whereby he was justified and blessed, and which Paul proclaimed as a standard and a model, was essentially an unyielding trust in God's promise. The same principle is taught in Hebrews 11, where faith is depicted as a spirit of obedient loyalty to God on the basis of trust in His promises, both general (the promise of reward, verse 6) and particular (such as the promise of a child to Sarah, who "counted him faithful who had promised," verse 11).

Where shall we find the promises which we are to trust? Abraham received God's promise by immediate revelation, but what of us, living nineteen centuries after immediate revelations ended? It must be emphasized that, if the Bible were not God's revealed Word in the sense explained in the opening section — if, that is, no one could be sure that everything which the Biblical writers say of God, God also says of Himself — we could not be sure either that any single statement in the Bible purporting to be a promise of God to Christian believers is really valid. No critical cross-examination on earth can tell us whether such statements are genuine divine commitments to which God has' pledged Himself to stand to all eternity, or whether the human writers were not perhaps astray in the words of promise which they put into the mouths of Jesus and his Father, and the assurances which they gave in God's name. If the canonical Scriptures were not God's revealed Word, but only a mere fallible human witness to God's Word, no present-day Christian could emulate Abraham's faith, because none could be sure that he had a single definite promise from God on which to rest. The historic evangelical concept of the life of faith as a matter of living and dying in the strength which God's promises give would then have to be thrown away as a beautiful pipedream. Those who jettison the evangelical concept of a totally trustworthy inspired Scripture must exchange the rational Biblical notion of faith as walking in the light of God for the irrational existential idea of faith as a leap in the dark, and must abandon the firm foundation of the divine promises for the yawning abyss of an empty nihilism.

THE COMMUNICATION
OF REVELATION
Kenneth S. Kantzer

Kenneth S. Kantzer

Kenneth S. Kantzer is Dean of the Trinity Evangelical Divinity School in Bannockburn, Deerfield, Illinois. From 1946 to 1963 he was a member of the Faculty of Wheaton College, where he held the Charles Deal Chair of Theology, and was Chairman of the Department of Bible and Philosophy, and Professor of Theology in the Graduate School. He holds the Ph.D. degree from Harvard University, and has pursued post-doctoral studies in the Universities of Göttingen and Basel.

Chapter III

THE COMMUNICATION
OF REVELATION

IN EVERY AGE OF THE CHRISTIAN CHURCH certain key issues become the dominant problems of the day. In the last century the idea of revelation has certainly proved to be such an issue. Even the current debate over the God-is-Dead movement is in reality not so much a discussion of the existence of God as it is of the revelation of God.[1] Archbishop William Temple does not exaggerate the situation when he writes: "The dominant problem of contemporary religious thought is the problem of revelation — Is there such a thing at all? If there is, what is its mode and form? Is it discoverable in all existing things or only in some? If in some, then in which? And by what principles are these selected as its vehicle? Where is it found? or believed to be found? What is its authority?"[2]

THE NATURE OF REVELATION

Divine revelation is often limited merely to the disclosure of truth or ideas. According to this understanding of divine revelation, God disclosed truths He wished men to know about Himself by dictating His messages to His prophets of the Old Testament and to Christ's apostles in the New Testament. Since the completion of the last book of the Bible, however, God has ceased to reveal Himself. All revelation for men today is, so to speak,

53

received "secondhand" by accurate copying and translation of the words dictated to the writers of Holy Scripture two or more millennia ago.[3]

In recent years this commonly held viewpoint has come under serious attack from almost every quarter. Objections generally center upon three lines of argumentation. First, it is argued that such an identification of divine revelation with the human words of the Bible is derogatory to God because it makes Him responsible for the imperfections imbedded in the Bible and necessary in all human statements of truth. Particularly, when the Bible is viewed as an inerrant book dictated by God, God must be held directly responsible for all moral shortcomings as well as for any historical and scientific inadequacies found in Scripture.[4]

In the second place, this traditional view is objectionable to many contemporary thinkers because it offers to man something less than personal encounter and personal communion with God Himself. It seems to place the focus of divine revelation upon a book or a set of truths stated in human language rather than upon the true object of man's devotion — God. It calls for a mere intellectual acceptance of these revealed truths instead of a personal communion and commitment to God. In short, it seems in a sort of deistic fashion to set a distance between God and contemporary man, bridged only by ancient documents that deprive man of any immediate and personal access to God Himself.[5]

Finally, this viewpoint is opposed on the simple grounds that in reality it is not Biblical. Those who ascribe to the Bible the honor of being a divine document, dictated by God to His prophets and apostles of old, so it is alleged, do the Bible a poor service because they are claiming for it a dubious honor which it does not claim for itself but rather repudiates on almost every page.[6]

The Contemporary View of Revelation

By contrast with this traditional viewpoint, many contemporary theologians agree that the true nature of divine revelation must be conceived quite differently. According to this more modern view the content of divine revelation is never a body of doctrine

or inspired truths such as are contained in the Bible. Rather,
divine revelation always has as its true object God Himself as a
person. Thus John Baillie, summing up what he believes to be
the view of most thinkers of the day, declares: "From a very
early time in the history of the church the tendency has manifested itself to equate divine revelation with a body of information which God communicates to man. We must rather think of
Him as giving Himself to us in communion. Our examination of
New Testament usage . . . confirms our conclusion that what is
revealed is not a body of information or doctrine. God does not
give us information by communication. He gives us Himself in
communion. It is not information about God that is revealed but
. . . God Himself."[7] Baillie is supported in his claims by no less
an authority than Kittel's *Dictionary of Theology*.[8] Indeed contemporary religious scholarship is all but unanimous in its agreement that revelation has as its object God as a person, not truth
or propositions about God.

Most contemporary theologians, likewise, are in agreement that
the method of divine revelation is not a dictation of truths to the
prophets and apostles of the Bible. Rather the divine method of
revelation consists of the mighty acts of God in nature, in history,
in the human soul, and above all, in Jesus Christ. Again John
Baillie speaks for many others when he writes, ". . . one of the
points in which there appears a remarkable breadth of agreement
in recent discussions about revelation [is] . . . that God reveals
himself in action — in the gracious activity by which he invades
the field of human existence and human history which is otherwise but a vain show empty and drained of meaning."[9]

The Bible, so Baillie and others argue, is essentially the story of
the acts of God. Other sacred books are composed of oracles
which purport to be timeless truths about universal being or timeless prescriptions for the conduct of life and worship, but the
Bible is mainly a record of what God has done.[10]

Finally, according to this modern concept of revelation, the
act of revelation is subjectively constituted. Revelation was not
completed in the past with the closing of the canon of Scripture.
Rather revelation keeps occurring continuously in the life of the
Church as God acts here and now to reveal Himself to His people.

Here again Baillie sums up the general view quite clearly: "We have seen that the divine act of revelation cannot be seen to be completed unless it is apprehended as such, just as I cannot be said to have revealed anything to you if you do not at all understand what I have desired to convey . . . It follows that God reveals Himself to me only in so far as I apprehend Him."[11]

THE TRUTH IN THIS CONTEMPORARY VIEW

A careful analysis of the Biblical and factual data indicates that the contemporary view of revelation as represented by Baillie is not wholly false. All Biblical revelation has God for its object. The Bible, for example, does not present man with a set of universal truths like the propositions of Euclid in geometry. Certainly no particular truths about God, such as the universal fatherhood of God, the universal brotherhood of man, and the supremacy of love (often cited as fundamental doctrines of the older liberal theology) are the focus of Biblical revelation. Isaiah in his vision did not merely see *that* God is holy. He saw the Lord sitting upon a throne high and lifted up (Isaiah 6). In Shiloh the Lord revealed Himself to Samuel (I Samuel 3:21). The object of Biblical revelation is God as a person.

Again, it is equally Biblical to assert, along with Baillie and other modern thinkers, that the ultimate goal of all divine revelation is not so much to make man wise as it is to bring him to direct encounter with God as a person, and to evoke from man the response of fellowship with and obedience to God. The Apostle Paul thus sets forth the goal of Biblical revelation not only for himself but for Christians of all times: "That I may be personally acquainted with Him" (Philippians 3:10, Greek).

Baillie likewise is on solid ground in noting that the Biblical revelation is imbedded in history. The long course of Biblical history is the story of what God has done for His people — "the righteous acts of Jehovah" (Micah 6:5).

Finally, the contemporary view rightly centers all Biblical revelation in Jesus Christ. The supreme act of divine revelation is the act by which God became incarnate in Jesus Christ and lived out for man His divine life on earth. "When the fulness of the time came, God sent forth his Son, born of a woman" (Galatians 4:4). "God . . . hath at the end of these days spoken unto us in his Son" (Hebrews 1:1, 2).

THE ERROR OF THE CONTEMPORARY VIEW

In spite of these splendid insights into the Biblical view of revelation stressed by much recent theology, Baillie and those who support his "Idea of Revelation" fall far short of the full Biblical viewpoint on this crucial question. The supremacy of the divine act of incarnation in Jesus Christ, for example, is not understood in its Biblical perspective. Most modern thinkers generally lump together all Biblical statements focusing upon Christ and assume that they exalt Christ as the supreme revelation of God. The Bible, on the contrary, preserves an important distinction between Christ as redeemer and Christ as revealer. Usually the Bible does not set forth the "mighty acts" of God as designed chiefly to reveal God as a person or to reveal truth about God. Their main purpose is salvatory — to deliver man from his predicament. Particularly in the case of Jesus Christ the Scriptures do not view Him primarily as the revealer of God but as the Saviour of man. The New Testament "gospel" is not news about the character of God or even about His attitude toward man. It is rather the news of an act of atonement provided for us objectively by God in Christ on the cross of Golgotha outside the city walls of Jerusalem.

Naturally these two aspects of the acts of God (revelation and salvation) are not separated from one another in the Biblical material. In both of these roles Jesus Christ is supreme. As Redeemer, however, Christ is not merely supreme over all other modes of redemption. His uniqueness is absolute. Other acts of God are simply preparatory and have no ultimate significance apart from the act of God in Jesus Christ. Like Christ, the prophets also spoke, but the prophets did not redeem. As a revealer, on the contrary, Christ's supremacy is only relative. His uniqueness lies in the completeness and finality of His revelation. Others spoke the word of God, but He was in truth God speaking.

The most significant error of the modern viewpoint is that it fails to understand the vast amount of Biblical material which clearly presents a revelation of truth. The importance of this neglect cannot be overestimated. Even the Gospel that Christ died for our sins (I Corinthians 15:3) is a trustworthy interpretation, not immediately observable from the act itself. Christ's death on the cross, for example, is a fact in human history. But as Paul Minear wisely remarks, "How could a bystander in Jerusalem watching one of the innumerable executions beyond the city wall detect that scene (the crucifixion) of Christ as one decisive for all history?"[12]

The immediate contemporaries who witnessed Christ's death on the cross did not automatically interpret it as a victory for law and order. Even by Christ's own disciples it was mourned as a defeat. It could with considerable justification have been interpreted as an example of dying for a principle. The resurrection, likewise, could have been interpreted as God's vindication of Jesus as really righteous and as wrongly condemned by the Jews. In the New Testament the Gospel was not the message that Christ died. Rather the Gospel was the good news that Christ died *for our sins* and rose again for our justification. It is the event plus the meaning or the significance of this event that together constitute the essential good news of the New Testament.

Biblical revelation thus becomes a blend of act and interpretation, both of which are essential to redemptive history as recorded in Scripture. As Oscar Cullman observes, "The act of interpretation based on revelation to the prophets is regarded as belonging to redemptive history itself. . . . This inclusion of the saving communication and the saving event is very essential for the New Testament."[13]

From a Biblical perspective, moreover, this communicated meaning or Word of God has the same objective status as do the acts of revelation to which Baillie refers. Vincent Taylor, accordingly, argues against Leonard Hodgson: "And if for our answer we go further and claim the aid of the Holy Spirit (to secure the right interpretation of uninterpreted acts of God), we cannot rule out the greater probability that the self-same Spirit guided prophet and apostle; and so we are back to the view that revelation may well be embodied in statements as well as in divine acts. On a priori grounds there is no compelling reason why revelation should be found in mighty acts of God but not in word. Indeed words can be a better medium of communication than events which need to be explained. Moreover, the explanation of events as mighty acts of God is itself an historical judgment, no doubt valid, but nevertheless exposed to all the uncertainties of such judgment. The truth is, we cannot avoid some theory of Biblical inspiration if we are to find a worthy doctrine of revelation."[14]

It is certainly clear that the Old Testament prophets understood their function not merely as recording the acts by which God had revealed Himself but also as stating truths which had been received by them from God as revelations of meaning. Their commission from God, as they conceived it, involved a commission to speak forth the divine Word which in fact God Himself was speaking through them. They were, as prophets, "mouthpieces for God" (Exodus 4:10-16).

C. H. Dodd correctly understands the Biblical and prophetic psychology when he writes: ". . . they (the Biblical writers) were not philosophers constructing a speculative theory from their observations of events. What they said was, 'Thus saith the Lord.' They firmly believed that God spoke to them, spoke to the inward ear in the spiritual sense. He spoke to them out of the events which they experienced. The interpretation which they offered was not invented by a process of thought. It was the meaning which they experienced in the events when their minds were open to God as well as open to the impact of outward facts. Thus the prophetic interpretation of history, and the impetus and direction which that gave to subsequent history were alike the word of God to men."[15]

The Old Testament, therefore, passes easily from the revelation of God as a person to the divine revelation of truth. In I Samuel 3:7, for example, both types of revelation are united in a single verse. Samuel did not yet know the Lord, neither was the Word of the Lord yet revealed unto him. Then the Lord spoke, and Samuel heard the Word of God spoken unto him. This revelation of divine truths accompanying the divine act is understood by the Old Testament writers as identifiable with an objective body of instructions. "The secret things belong unto Jehovah our God; but the things that are revealed belong unto us and to our children forever, that we may do all the words of this law [note the root meaning of 'Torah' as 'instruction']" (Deuteronomy 29:29).

In spite of the claims of Oepke in *The Theological Dictionary*, the New Testament clearly supports the same view of a divine revelation of truths.[16] Matthew 11:22 reminds us that God revealed the truth about His own future judgments. Paul declares that the oracles of God were committed to the Jews (Romans 3:2). In the third chapter of Ephesians the same apostle refers to the revealed truth that Jews and Gentiles are to be one body (Ephesians 3:6). In Matthew 16:16, 17 the revealed truth is that Jesus Christ is the Son of God.

Walter Bauer in his *Standard Greek-English Lexicon of the New Testament* lists ten usages of the Greek verb "to reveal" as referring to ideas of truth, and cites three instances where the noun form of *apokalypsis* indicates truth to be the object of revelation.[17]

When other words besides the Old Testament *galah* and the New Testament *apokalypsis* are considered, the Biblical idea of revelation of truth becomes abundantly clear. God warns, causes to know, causes to learn, instructs, foretells, testifies, and, especially, says. The last is probably used more frequently than any other word in Scripture to convey the idea of revelation, and pointedly demands as its meaning the verbal and propositional form of truth revelation. "Thus saith Jehovah" is the earmark of genuine Biblical prophecy. Almost equally common and likewise stressing the verbal nature of revelation as giving of truth are such familiar phrases as "The Word of the Lord" (King James Version), the "utterance" of Jehovah, and the "burden" of Jehovah.[18]

The classic Biblical passage dealing with revelation and related concepts of divine communication is I Corinthians 2:9-16:

> But as it is written,
>> Things which eye saw not, and ear heard not,
>> And which entered not into the heart of man,
>> Whatsoever things God prepared for them that love Him.
> But unto us God revealed them through the Spirit: for the Spirit searcheth all things, yea, the deep things of God. For who among men knoweth the things of a man, save the spirit of the man, which is in him? even so the things of God none knoweth, save the Spirit of God. But we received,

not the spirit of the world, but the spirit which is from God; that we might know the things that were freely given to us of God. Which things also we speak, not in words which man's wisdom teacheth, but which the Spirit teacheth; combining spiritual things with spiritual words. Now the natural man receiveth not the things of the Spirit of God: for they are foolishness unto him; and he cannot know them, because they are spiritually judged. But he that is spiritual judgeth all things, and he himself is judged of no man. For who hath known the mind of the Lord, that he should instruct him? But we have the mind of Christ.

In this passage the flow of Paul's logic is inescapably clear. God has certain plans for those who love Him. These plans are necessarily unknown to the mind of man and undiscoverable by man through any investigation of his own, presumably because they are the personal decision of the free and sovereign God and could not be inferred as necessary either from God's nature or His previous works. Just as only man knows what is in his own mind, so the Spirit of God alone knows what is in His divine mind. Furthermore, just as man can choose to communicate what he knows in his own mind to another mind, so the Spirit of God, who alone knows fully the truth of His own plans and purposes, can choose to convey these otherwise inaccessible truths to the minds of His chosen apostles. The process whereby this communication of divine truth takes place is specifically labelled revelation. This truth-revelation "stood revealed." The verb in the Greek aorist intensifies the past and objective nature of the revelation. When this revelation of truth is communicated by God to His apostle, the apostle in turn can speak words as he is guided and enabled by God. Similarly, those to whom he ministers may receive the same truth-revelation which the apostle himself had previously received from the mind of God.

The Biblical view of divine revelation is thus well summarized by James Barr: "Direct verbal communication between God and particular men on particular occasions, is, I believe, an inescapable fact of the Bible and of the Old Testament in particular. God can speak specific verbal messages when he wills to men of his choice. But for this, if we follow the way in which the Old Testament presents the incidents, there would have been no call of Abraham, no exodus, no prophecy. Direct communications from God to man have fully as much claim to be called the core of the tradition as has revelation of events in history. If we persist in saying that this direct specific communication must be subsumed under the revelation of events in history and taken as a subsidiary interpretation of the latter, I shall say that we are abandoning the Bible's own presentation of the matter for another which is apologetically more comfortable."[19]

To sum up then, Biblical revelation provides both act or event revelation, and truth or idea revelation. The meaning of the mighty revelatory acts of God including the crowning act of all, God incarnate in Jesus Christ, is not a humanly drawn conclusion based on astute observation of these acts. Rather the meaning of the act is itself also divine revelation — God interprets for man His own divine acts. This revelatory word is given by God to man in just as objective a form as are the acts of God in history. These revelations of truth represent God's interpretations. They are God's meaning of events in history, God's truth for men. Truth-revelation in fact constitutes an enormously important segment of Biblical revelation. It not only accompanies act-revelation to interpret the meaning of the act, but truth-revelation predicts the acts, and contains and canonizes the story or record of the divine act-revelation. Truth-revelation has, therefore, every whit as much right to be considered of the essence of Biblical revelation as do "mighty (wordless) acts." Biblical revelation is a continuous independent unity of act-revelation and truth-revelation.

General Revelation

Revelation is commonly divided into two basically different areas. General revelation (or natural revelation or natural theology) is contrasted with special revelation (or supernatural revelation or revealed theology). General revelation refers to those communications available for all mankind, not merely to the chosen people of God. Special revelation, by contrast, is that revelation which relates specifically to the redemptive program of God given to a particular people, Israel in the Old Testament and the New Testament church in the New Testament.

In the Reformation period Luther and Calvin reacted against

the strong emphasis on natural revelation inherited by the church from the medieval theologian, Thomas Aquinas. They held man to be totally depraved (i.e., in intellect as well as in will). Luther spoke of the image of God as lost and of reason as the devil's bride. Natural man, therefore, cannot discover a true philosophy. Yet Luther did not deny altogether the existence of valid general revelation. For him, man is still man. He can reason about earthly things. Luther disparaged only man's subjective capacity to grasp this general revelation and to put it to positively good uses apart from regeneration and special revelation. He spoke glowingly of a natural revelation objectively given by God.[20]

Calvin, on the other hand, argued that the image of God is defaced, but not destroyed. Unsaved man cannot, as a result, reach all the truth he might have reached had he remained unfallen. Like Luther, thus, he spoke glowingly of what man ought to be able to see in nature. He insisted on the objective validity of the natural evidences for theism. He noted that some unregenerate men see important truth about God. But he argued that unregenerate man does not avail himself of these to come to any right knowledge of God.[21]

Post-reformation Protestants of orthodox persuasion, whether in the Lutheran, Reformed or Anglican camp, generally held to the validity of natural revelation. They argued, however, that it is not adequate for man as a sinner because it is of no avail in providing for man a way of salvation. Rather, it is useful to explain God's righteous condemnation of the heathen; it serves as a missionary point of contact in presenting the Gospel to the heathen; and it is an explanation of false religions, which are in part based upon man's perversion of a primitive special revelation of God.[22]

In recent decades the Neo-orthodox "Revolt against Reason" has taken an extreme turn on this issue.[23] In repudiating the rationalistic and deistic tendencies of nineteenth century philosophy of religion, Neo-orthodox thinkers in general repudiate the validity of any natural revelation. Karl Barth, for example, in his famous treatise, *Nein*, warns against all use of natural evidences as a denial of grace and as the attempt on man's part to contribute to his own salvation or righteousness by intellectual works.[24] Even Brunner does not conceive of a divine revelation in nature in the sense that man may draw conclusions about God's existence and nature from the data of the physical universe. According to Brunner nature serves as the occasion through which God speaks to man immediately and personally by His Holy Spirit. As viewed by Brunner, however, such general revelation never possesses saving significance for the sinner.[25]

Scriptural teaching regarding the revelation of God in nature may be summarized as follows:

1. There is a natural revelation of God in the sense of data in nature which can only be fitted together in coherent fashion on the supposition that God does actually exist. This will not provide, however, a natural theology in the Thomistic sense that the knowledge thus obtained is sufficient to build an adequate philosophy of life for a man who had not sinned. The revelation of God in nature was never adequate for Adam even before he fell. The fall brought an end to continuous and immediate special revelation. There is, therefore, no complete *natural* system of theology adequate for man's needs apart from sin.

2. The evidence for theism is altogether adequate to show that God is. From a scriptural point of view all objections such as "How can the finite arrive at the infinite?" or "How can we know that we can trust our reason?" or "How do we know that the world is not eternal?" are in every case invalid. From the scriptural point of view the data of the universe about us bring to all men the fact of the presence of God in as inescapable fashion as the sun during its course across the heavens sheds its light and heat upon man everywhere on the earth (Psalm 19:6). In Romans 1:20 Paul presented data which, ever since the creation of the world, are sufficient, as data, to lead man to a knowledge of God's eternal power and of His essential deity. Romans 2:14 and 15 explicitly assert, that, apart from any knowledge of the special revelation, man would still know the moral law and his obligation to God. The entire point of these passages is that the evidences are valid and, because of this, man can be justly condemned. He ought to see, and if he does not see, it is only because he *will* not see.

From a scriptural point of view all objections against the

validity of these arguments, therefore, are invalid. The lack is neither in the evidences nor in the finiteness of man.

The objection that nature reveals God only as a string tied around a small boy's finger to remind him to get a loaf of bread is erroneous. The Biblical point is not that nature is a memorandum of a God knowable only on other grounds, but rather that precisely on these grounds God could be known by man if he will to do so. Since man does not wish to accept natural revelation, he is rightly condemned if he does not see God. The Bible presents the situation as one in which the evidences show to all right thinking minds that God exists, and this body of evidence would be utterly convincing to all who are thinking rightly.

3. From the Biblical data, moreover, it is not a "mere something," but the existence of a being properly called God that is proved, as Romans 1:18 ff. shows with particular clarity. The "hidden things" of God are displayed by means of the physical creation. That is, in nature God reveals His divine attributes. These divine attributes are then further defined as His eternal power and Godhead.

The statement that God's existence is provable, but not His attributes, is both nonsense and unbiblical. What is it to prove the existence of God but to prove the existence of a being who possesses such attributes as make it right to call that which is proved by the name "God" rather than "stone" or "angel"? Obviously, if we would limit our thinking to Biblical terms, we must not read too much into the phrases, the "eternal power and Godhead," or the "law written on the heart."

4. The formal theistic arguments as separate demonstrations are not found in the Scripture in direct fashion. Scripture does, however, point to the fact of the created universe and demands the conclusion of theism. These facts lie in the areas commonly designated by the terms cosmological, teleological, moral, and revelational. The type of argumentation is strictly inductive. From the data available in the physical nature (Romans 1 and Psalm 19), from the evidence of history (Acts 14, 17), and from the facts of moral consciousness (Romans 2:14, 15) man ought to be able to draw the conclusion, coherent only with these bodies of data, namely the existence of a supreme being properly

called God, to whom we are morally responsible. Note that the
Scripture does not state that each of these arguments demands
theism. Rather, the whole of the data is adequate to establish
the existence of deity.

5. These evidences from nature alone, apart from special revelation, are sufficient as evidences to lead us to a knowledge of the
God of the Bible; but they are not sufficient to lead us to all we
need to know about the God of the Bible. For example, they
do not show us the Trinity or that God loves us in spite of our
sin. As sinners we need to know these things, but they cannot
be gleaned from natural revelation. On the other hand, the data
do not "point" us away from the God of the Bible. Quite the
contrary, the suggestion that they lead to *a* God but not *the*
God is decidedly unscriptural, for it obscures what the evidence is
intended to do and what it will do when rightfully employed.
The proof for this may be seen in the scriptural recognition of
exactly what the heathen did with the data of the natural revelation and wherein lay their condemnation. On the basis of the
data the heathen actually were led to the knowledge of the true
God. To their condemnation, however, they endeavored to crush
out of their minds this knowledge. They created for themselves
(*contrary* to what the data were intended to do and what they
could do if they were used rightly) the false image of a god of
man's own vain imagination. In doing this the heathen are reprehensible not for faithful adherence to the data but for failing to
follow the data. They refused to come to the right conclusions
(which the data, properly interpreted, required) but wilfully
perverted the data so as to arrive at wrong conclusions. They
are responsible, therefore, and are justly condemned because they
refused to draw the conclusions required by the evidence, and
also because they sought to push out of their minds even these
partially valid conclusions they achieved. Worst of all, of course,
they failed to act in ways appropriate to the truths which were
available for them.

6. Sin has affected this revelation objectively by the curse
upon the earth (Genesis 3:17-19; Romans 8:20-22), and by man's
perversion of his own consciousness (Romans 3:1-10). Nevertheless the objective revelation is still wholly adequate to show

that God is, that men are responsible to God, are sinners standing under the divine judgment, and need to turn to God for more light. Scripture, accordingly, speaks not merely of a past ideal but of a present and continuous situation in which the revelatory data are still valid in spite of man's fall and the curse upon the earth.

According to Romans 1:18 the data became available at creation and ever since then have remained available. Psalm 19 states that the sun of divine revelation now shines on all. It is true that the curse upon the earth affects the facts of the external world and also man's moral nature; therefore they do not reveal God so clearly as they otherwise might. Yet sufficient light now shines so that man could see God if he only would.

7. Sin has also affected the revelation subjectively. Because of sin the observer of revelation is unable, apart from the grace of illumination, to see as he ought what is objectively manifested. According to the Bible the unbeliever is never one who is really clever enough to see that the evidences do not prove God's existence; but he is morally reprehensible for failing to see what the evidences clearly point to and what he very well could see if he were only willing. Man as a sinner has an anti-God bias, which in some men is self-consciously expressed but in other cases (indeed in most cases) lies unrecognized in the subconscious mind of the unbeliever.

The noëtic effect of sin is not uniform through the entire range of human knowledge. In some areas the unbeliever may think as clearly or even more cogently than the believer (Luke 16:8). From this variableness there is evident a law of proportional rationality: *the nearer a man gets to the vital core of his obedience to God, the greater is the corruption of his thinking due to sin.*

8. This revelation of God in nature is supplemented by a general supernatural revelation of God. Through this revelation every soul is confronted personally and individually by God to convict him of his sin and of God's righteous judgment and condemnation upon him (John 16:8, 9), and to call all men everywhere to repentance and decision (John 1:9).

Every soul, therefore, must face God personally in this life and is brought to decision on the basis of God's general revelation and on the basis of personal encounter with God. This decision may not terminate on exactly the same point with different individuals, but ultimately it always terminates upon God's revelation of Himself and of His will to which men must say "yes," or "no."

9. In spite of man's incapacity in and of himself to see what he ought to see, the evidences for God and His truth ought to be presented to unbelievers to lead them to faith, and to believers to confirm their faith. Examples of this are found in Acts 14 and 17 and in Romans 1 and 2 (addressed primarily to believers but certainly also to an unbelieving minority). The chapters of Romans are not merely a Pauline theodicy for the believer, but they represent also a direct argument for the divine revelation and man's righteous condemnation addressed to the heathen, as Paul's use of the second person of direct address clearly shows. This necessity for presenting the data of general revelation parallels exactly the situation with reference to special revelation (Luke 1:1-4; John 5:39, 40; 20:30, 31; Acts 1:1-5; I Corinthians 15:1-11), in which the apostles call the unbeliever to repentance and faith on the basis of facts which they set forth and substantiate by adequate evidence.

10. By God's common grace the unbeliever is not necessarily deprived of all the knowledge of God. He may, for example, have many correct ideas about God and man's relationship to God which he holds with varying degrees of certitude as human opinions — so called *Fides Humana* by the older theologians. Such ideas include the existence of the true God (Romans 1:20, 21; James 2:19), that this God ought to be worshiped (Acts 17: 26, 27), the moral law (Romans 2:14, 15), and even the Christian plan of redemption (II Peter 2:21). What the unbeliever lacks is a knowledge of his acceptance or personal fellowship with God, which he cannot know because it does not yet exist. He lacks also a factual knowledge of truth about God in a proper setting; that is, a properly related knowledge held as an abiding conviction of the whole soul. This latter kind of knowledge of God is impossible as a mere act of human intellect or volition. It is a divine creation (*Fides Divina*) worked upon the whole

human soul by the miracle of God's Spirit (Colossians 3:10; I Corinthians 2:10, 13, 15, 16).

SPECIAL REVELATION

Natural revelation, valid and useful though it may be, is, nevertheless, not enough. For sinful man to know God rightly, special or supernatural revelation is essential.

Man's need for special revelation lies first of all in his inability to understand and appreciate the revelation of God in nature. Special revelation, therefore, provides for man an illumination so that he may better utilize natural revelation. It does this by bringing to man the Gospel of his redemption in Christ and thereby serving as the divine instrument in regeneration and sanctification. Regenerate man then becomes capable of reading the "Book of Nature" rightly. Special revelation thus restores natural revelation to its pristine glory and, as Calvin quaintly puts it, enables one to read the book of nature with glasses on so that he may see what is really there and was always available, but which he has incorrectly understood because of his own spiritual astigmatism.[26]

This is not to say that man needs special revelation only so that he may read the natural revelation rightly. In accordance with His sovereign plan, God made man for Himself to live with Him in continuous unbroken fellowship. Indeed, direct divine communication formed a "natural" element in man's pre-fallen existence (Genesis 3:8). Special revelation was no afterthought introduced to circumvent the fall of man, but was a part of the original divine economy. Only as a result of the curse and expulsion from the garden did such immediate converse between men and God become "special" (Genesis 3:24). Special revelation, therefore, not only reinstates natural revelation by enabling redeemed men to read the "book of nature"; it also transcends the "natural" revelation by furnishing man with more information than is even ideally obtainable in nature. This is particularly true of the revelation of a God of love. Christ, for example, gives us a better understanding of the love of God than could possibly be inferred from the natural world. One touch of His hand laid

on a bruised body or on blind eyes makes the divine love shine
forth as nature never could.[27]

After the fall, of course, man discovered his deepest need to be
a way of salvation from sin. Sin rendered the natural revelation
completely inadequate for the sinner's good. From the "book
of nature" we might learn that God is great and good and loving;
but God is merciful and good whether He condemns or forgives.
Certainly no man could ever rest in the assurance that he was
safe in placing his trust in the divine mercy apart from a special
revelation of the promise of forgiveness.[28]

In summary, therefore, special revelation is God's gift of grace
to sinful man in order (1) to restore to him the benefits of the
natural and general revelation given to man originally and, far
more important, (2) to bring to him the good news of God's
redemptive work in and through Jesus Christ. This divine program of the ages represents, of course, God's eternal plan undertaken for His own glory in order to bring ultimate blessing and
good to the race of man.

In accordance with this divine plan for mankind, God selected
a particular people who became the object of His special grace
and revelation. Eventually this revelatory work of God was restricted to the nation of Israel and to one particular family
within this nation. Any limitations of the special revelation, of
course, do not flow from religious exclusivism but from the
divine plan. Ultimately God chose Israel not for Israel's sake.
By His special revelation to Israel, He purposed to bring redemption to all the families of the earth (Genesis 12:1-3). Biblical
particularism is based solidly on a divine universalism as to the
plan of God for men.

Mysterious figures, like Melchizedek, Jethro, and Balaam occasionally appear in the Bible record and subsequently disappear altogether from sacred history, leaving no trace behind
them. Having experienced divine special revelation outside the
bounds of God's covenant people, they find their significance for
the divine plan to bring universal redemption only in their relationship to the chosen people of God. Their very existence,
however, serves as a needed reminder that one dare not absolutize
the restriction of divine special revelation to those whose history
is recorded in the Bible.

The methods by which God chose to reveal Himself specially to man are ordinarily subsumed under two heads: (1) the divine (wordless) acts in human history and (2) the divine word of truth. A careful analysis of Biblical data concerning revelation has made clear that a truly Biblical understanding of divine revelation includes both of these types. God has really acted in history, and God has really spoken His truth to man by direct verbal communication.

REVELATION BY THE "MIGHTY ACTS OF GOD IN HISTORY"

Biblical references to special revelation cannot be disassociated from divine miracle. Unfortunately the contemporary cliché "mighty acts" of God, beclouds the Biblical perspective because it skirts the issue of a supernatural miracle.[29] From a truly Biblical viewpoint, however, God reveals Himself *specially* by means of acts of immediate divine power (*dunamis*). The work of special revelation involves acts which cannot be explained on the same basis as God's ordinary works in nature and in human history. The significance of the Biblical miracles does not lie in the fact that man sees in any "natural" event a meaning not suggested by other events. Or, to put the matter another way, the *special* character of the "mighty act" does not basically consist of the increased insight man gleans from it. The significance of the Biblical miracle is to be found primarily in that God is acting directly. For the Biblical writer a miracle is an event worked by the immediate exercise of the divine energy and intended as a sign or attestation.

To suggest that for the ancient Jews of Bible times *all* acts were immediate acts of God is to miss altogether the Biblical perspective. Biblical miracles are events or "wonders" unexplainable merely on ordinary grounds, which, therefore, are "signs" of the divine presence and of His immediate and sovereign "power." Virgins do not bear children. Man does not separate vast bodies of water at a word of command. Dead bodies do not come back to life. But God can do all these things, and Biblical miracles are the acts by which He does what is impossible to nature or to man.

In the Old Testament the great central miracle was the deliverance of the people of God from Egypt. In the New Testament the central miracle is the resurrection of Jesus Christ from the dead. In both Old and New Testaments miracles are signs intended to testify to the supernatural hand of God in His special revelation.[30]

Supplementing these external miracles by which God acted within the framework of the natural world are internal revelations, by means of which God worked immediately upon the minds of men. These frequently took the form of dreams and visions. In such revelations the divine presence might manifest itself merely in wordless images. At other times the revelation takes the form of direct communication of a verbal character.

Frequently it is difficult to determine from the Biblical data when a verbal communication of divine truth took place only in the mind of the recipient of revelation, or whether there was an objective presentation of the divine Word. The objective character of the verbal revelation is certainly presented in the voice in the garden, the call of Samuel, or the voice from heaven at the baptism of Jesus. The same external presentation of the divine revelation occasionally appears in the form of direct writing, the most notable of which is the giving of the Ten Commandments by the finger of God.

Beginning with the Old Testament non-writing prophets and continuing intermittently into the New Testament, God selected certain men through whom He gave specific verbal messages for His people. The method of Biblical prophecy was not dictation, but certainly it came nearer to this mode of revelation than anything except the direct speech and writing referred to above. The entire activity of the prophet is concentrated upon the receiving of the message of God. He speaks not that which he is motivated to speak from the depths of his own soul, but he speaks by a special instigation of the divine Spirit working upon him and through him, so that what he speaks is the divine message and not that which is necessarily his own (II Peter 1:19-21).

On the other hand, Biblical prophecy must be distinguished from the dementia of pagan prophecy in which the human prophet lost his own consciousness and spoke as though from a trance. Except for the reference to Saul (I Samuel 19:24) which can hardly be reckoned as normative for our understanding of Biblical prophecy, the Biblical prophet is fully alert and is consciously aware of what he is doing. He is, indeed, active both in the securing and in the production of the divine message. The significant factor in Biblical prophecy, however, is that the prophet is active to receive and transmit but not to initiate or conceptualize by his own intelligence or will the idea he proclaims. God alone is the originator of the revealed message. He conveys it through His prophet by internal suggestion, the precise psychological mechanics of which are never clearly explained in the Biblical material.[31]

Much of the prophetic revelation was intended only for the moment and did not find its way into the permanent body of written prophecy or Holy Scriptures. Some of it, however, is recorded in Scripture and became normative for the people of God down through the centuries. In one sense Holy Scripture is but the valid written record by which God preserved His revelations in whatever form they originally came.

In the non-prophetic portions of the Old Testament and in the scriptural record of these prophetic utterances, the methodology of inspiration is quite different and pursues a pattern characteristic of almost the entire body of New Testament literature. Here one may discern a kind of dual authorship of the documents of Holy Scripture. All Scripture (or every passage of Scripture) is divinely "breathed out by God" (II Timothy 3: 16). What the scriptural passage teaches is as a whole and in all of its parts "the word of God" (Mark 7:13). Of any portion it can be said that "God says" what the human author of Scripture has written (Matthew 19:1-6; Acts 1:16; 28:25; Ephesians 4:8; Hebrews 1:1-8). In a legitimate sense, therefore, every word of the written scripture is the written Word of God because it has God as its ultimate author. The value of Scripture for man derives primarily from the fact that it is not merely man's word, possessing only human authority and liable to error; but rather it is God's Word and thereby inherently possessed of divine authority, worthy of binding the conscience of man, and characterized by that unbroken truth and dependability which only God's Word could possess.

The Biblical claims that Holy Scripture was produced by God are not in the least restricted to the use of the word "inspiration" itself. The English word "inspiration" is used only once in the New Testament, and in this instance it is a trifle misleading. It suggests a breathing into the Scripture, whereas the root meaning of the Greek word (*theopneustia*) is better translated divine "spiration" or "expiration" of Holy Scripture. The doctrine of inspiration indicated in II Timothy 3:16 is a divine productivity of Holy Scripture which renders it trustworthy and thus a reliable guide for the thought and life of the Christian. This divine *"spiration,"* of course, applies to Scripture, that is, *not to unwritten concepts or concepts which become written* but to what is *written.* The written symbols of concepts as found in the autographs of the apostles and prophets are the products of God. In different words II Peter 1:20 and 21 point up the same truth: "Holy men of God spake as they were moved by the Holy Ghost." So also Paul in I Corinthians 2:13 declares that he speaks forth the revelation which God had given to him ". . . not in words which man's wisdom teacheth, but which the Spirit teacheth." This divine "spiration" of the apostolic witness to Christ is explained as a divine authorship and responsibility, paralleling exactly the human authorship of the Bible so as to give to the written human word of Scripture divine authorship and therefore divine authority.

Although the material indicating the human side of the scriptural writing is not so prominent as that relating to its divine side, still the teaching of Scripture on this point also is amazingly clear, once it is seen in its proper perspective.

In Luke 1:1-4 the author writes that he has a human motive for selecting and collecting his materials in order that he might reassure one who has learned something of the story of the Christian faith, but has not been fully convinced of its truthfulness. He concludes his introduction to the Gospel by listing his human qualifications for his ability to write in such a way as to accomplish this purpose.

Likewise in John 20:30 and 31 the apostle tells us that Christ did many things during His earthly ministry. The whole could not possibly be written in any book, but he has deliberately chosen to record these materials in his Gospel to lead men to the conclusion that Jesus Christ is the Messiah, and that by putting their trust in Him they might have everlasting life.

In the production of God's written Word, Biblical writers use many uninspired sources; the book of Chronicles alone refers to twelve.[32] Many of these sources could not possibly be extant books of the Scripture because they relate details not to be found in the canonical books. The book of Kings refers to the Acts of Solomon,[33] cites the Book of the Chronicles of the Kings of Judah fifteen times,[34] and the Chronicles of the Kings of Israel seventeen times,[35] besides referring to numerous eyewitness accounts such as must have been preserved from histories of Elijah, Elisha and Micaiah.

In the scriptural teaching as to its own nature, the Holy Scriptures of Old and New Testaments are a human record of the acts and words of God; but these very written documents are also, as a whole and in all their parts, the very Word of God. As the New Testament makes plain, what the Scriptures say or what the Biblical author says, God Himself or His Spirit says.

The Biblical formula, "The prophet by the Spirit says," indicates the twofold authorship pervading the whole of the written Scripture. All of Scripture was produced by human authors whose writings reflect throughout the individual personality and linguistic habits of each particular Biblical author. At the same time the Spirit of God so worked upon the Biblical author that what he wrote is also exactly that message which God wishes to convey to man. Biblical inspiration may be defined, therefore, as that work of the Holy Spirit by which, without setting aside their personalities and literary or human faculties, God so guided the authors of Scripture as to enable them to write exactly the words which convey His truth to men, and in doing so preserved their judgments from error in the original manuscripts. Or, inspiration is the work of the Holy Spirit by which He employed the instrumentality of the whole personality, literary talents, and various faculties of their human authors to constitute the words of the Biblical autographs as His written Word to men and, therefore, of divine authority and without error in faith (what we ought to believe) and practice (what we ought to do).

The focus of Biblical teaching regarding Scripture, it is important to note, is not upon the method of inspiration or upon the inner relationship between the divine and the human activity in the production of Scripture. The Biblical emphasis regarding Scripture is upon the result of its inspiration, that is, upon Scripture as a product of God's activity in such a sense that He secures in Scripture what He desires in order to convey satisfactorily the ideas He wishes to communicate. This divine guidance in its production gives to Scripture its inherent divine authority and truthfulness. The burden of scriptural teaching regarding Biblical inspiration, therefore, is not the method but the fact of its divine "spiration" and its consequent authority and complete trustworthiness.

This divine authorship and consequent authority of the Scripture is complete, that is, coterminous with the whole of the written Scripture. Scripture, therefore, is constituted both inerrant (free from any judgments which in the sense intended are not true) and infallible (incapable of setting forth statements or judgments which in the sense intended are untrue).

Certainly the Bible provides no doctrine of a criterion for accepting parts of the Biblical teaching as coming from God and rejecting other parts as not coming from God, and hence of being without divine authority. Suggested principles are in every case extra-Biblical, subjectively or rationalistically grounded, and without justification from the teaching of Scripture itself. The doctrine of Scripture about Scripture is: All of it is to be believed.

JESUS CHRIST AS DIVINE REVELATION

The consummating mode of revelation in all of Scripture, which serves to tie all other modes together, is the person of Jesus Christ. Jesus Christ differs from other modes in that He is not so much a mode of the divine communication as He is the divine being Himself, communicating to man directly in and through His incarnation in the human race. Jesus Christ combines both the act of revelation and the word of revelation. He is God acting; and when He speaks, He is, in turn, God speaking with divine authority and divine infallibility.

Jesus Christ, moreover, is the focal center of all of the scriptural teaching. As He Himself testified of the Holy Scriptures:

"They testify of me" (John 5:39). This is not to be construed, as some modern writers do, as a sort of sieve through which we sift the material of the Bible in order to discover what parts of it are acceptable to us and what parts are not. One may not, as they suggest, receive those parts of Scripture which reflect Jesus Christ and reject the other parts. Rather, in the mind of Jesus and certainly in the Biblical view of itself, the whole of Holy Scripture, rightly interpreted, points to Jesus Christ and to the benefits of God's redemption in and through Him. Jesus Christ becomes *not a critical principle* to divide between the acceptable and the unacceptable, but a *hermeneutical principle* to enable us to understand fully and adequately what is the true meaning of the Scripture. One may not project a view of Christ extraneous to the Bible or derived from some inner kernel of the Bible, and then judge the rest of the Bible by this. Rather he receives the Bible and the whole of the Bible as divine revelation, and finds in that whole all that he needs to know about Christ and His meaning for us.[36]

In view of this principle, no rigid boundary can be placed between the mode of revelation that is Scripture and the mode that is Jesus Christ. We learn of Jesus Christ from the Scripture. The Jesus Christ who is our Lord and ultimate revelation of God is the Jesus Christ of Holy Scripture and none other. Scripture itself is in turn validated by Jesus Christ. It is the final guide for faith and for all action on the basis of the Lord's authority. In the light of Jesus' own views about Scripture and particularly in the light of His commands concerning Scripture given to His disciples, no true follower of Jesus Christ dares to do otherwise. Either Christ is Lord and one obeys His command to acknowledge the divine authority of Holy Scripture, or he falsely calls Him Lord because in his rejection of scriptural authority he rejects also Christ's authority.

THE RECEPTION OF REVELATION

The crowning work of God in the communication of His revelation to man is the internal work of the Holy Spirit which enables him to accord to all the revelatory acts and words of God their proper significance. In the Biblical vocabulary various terms and phrases are employed to describe this work of the Spirit. Man tries or tests the spirits to discern whether or not they are holy. His ears are opened and he hears; scales drop from his blind eyes and he is able to see; his conscience is pressed; his heart burns within him; his mind is enlightened and the vision of God is unveiled for him.

This work of the Spirit is most frequently called illumination. By illumination is meant the work of the Holy Spirit by which He enables man to recognize the divine revelation in act or word, and to respond to it with appropriate acceptance and trust.[37]

Illumination thus enables the believer to see that the Bible was produced by inspiration of God, and as such has complete divine authority over his faith and practice. It leads him to a correct interpretation as he opens himself to the meaning of its words in their context. It helps abstractly in making the correct application of Scripture to thought and life. Finally, in existential situations the illumination of the Spirit enables the individual believer to apply the truths of Scripture as God's present word to the soul. This is the great truth suggested by the cliché, the Bible "becomes the word of God." Although this truth has been overemphasized and placed in a dangerously subjective context by the Neo-orthodox theologians, it expresses, nevertheless, a solidly Biblical understanding of the relation between the Spirit of God and the text of Scripture. It needs to be supplemented and adequately safeguarded, of course, by the corresponding work of revelation and inspiration.

By revelation God communicates Himself and His truth to man through His (wordless) acts and through His (acts of communication by) words. The Bible provides the record of these acts of God in the past; and thus it may be said correctly: "The Bible *contains* the Word of God."

By inspiration, God also saw fit to provide His own divinely guided prophetic and apostolic Word about the revelatory acts and words of God given in history. Scripture, therefore, is the divinely guaranteed record of God's words and acts provided by human authors who were so motivated, guided and taught by the Spirit that they convey exactly that which God wishes to say to men. It may thus also be said quite correctly: "The Bible *is* the Word of God."

By illumination, God enables men to recognize the Jesus Christ of Holy Scripture as their present living Lord and Saviour, and to recognize and receive Holy Scripture for what it is — God's Word, which stands in objective and permanent written form. By means of it Christ chooses in grace to exercise His lordship over the heart and mind of His disciples, and He speaks His truth and His gracious will to men today wherever and whenever they will hear His voice in the pages of Holy Writ. It may thus, finally, be said correctly and with full Biblical warrant: "The Bible *becomes* the Word of God."

The great truths of revelation and inspiration have always been a united and integral part of the catholic doctrine of Holy Scripture and of divine revelation. Necessarily joined to them to complete the Biblical perspective is the doctrine of divine illumination. By the reformation theologians and by the classical theologians of the eighteenth and nineteenth centuries this important doctrine was generally discussed at the end of the "system" under the *loci*, subjective response of faith and the means of divine grace. By the twentieth century writers of orthodox persuasion, the Biblical doctrine of illumination has been largely neglected.[38]

The importance of the doctrine of divine illumination of Holy Scripture and its role as a means of grace to the believer can scarcely be exaggerated. It transforms the Bible from a "paper pope" to the "living voice of the Spirit." The same Holy Spirit who spoke in time past by His prophets and apostles now speaks directly to contemporary man. Without the illumination of the Holy Spirit all direct personal relationship to God would be lost. The Bible would be merely an ancient document setting forth truths given by God to people who lived millennia ago. With the illumination of the Holy Spirit, the simple believer in Christ meets God immediately as the living God speaks to him personally in the pages of the Bible.

At the same time, the faithful disciple of Jesus Christ is kept from the morass of a subjectivism in which the divine voice is only the echo of his own hallucination. God's voice to man is not incomprehensible or unrecognizable, but is knowable and identifiable in the divinely inspired words of Holy Scripture. God's truth is not some humanly devised thought suggested by the Biblical text; nor is it some hidden meaning which must be derived from the text by esoteric methods of selecting the kernel of divine truth from the outer husk of human words. In every mode of its expression, the Bible conveys through understandable language the mind and will of God.

THE PROBLEM
OF COMMUNICATION
R. Laird Harris

R. Laird Harris

R. Laird Harris is Dean of Covenant Theological Seminary in St. Louis, Missouri. He is the author of *Introductory Hebrew Grammar, Inspiration and Canonicity of the Bible*, and a contributor to *Inspiration and Interpretation*, and to *The Wycliffe Commentary*. He holds the degree of Ph.D. from Dropsie College for Hebrew and Cognate Languages.

Chapter IV

THE PROBLEM
OF COMMUNICATION

A HINDU PHILOSOPHER, contemplating the movement of ants around an ant hill, was struck by the thought that he could communicate with the ants only if he could assume the nature of an ant. The anecdote illustrates some of the factors in the problem of communication. First, there must be a communicator; next, there must be a congruity of some sort between the one communicating and the one he is addressing; and for rational, effective communication there must be some medium and some admitted principles of discourse.

The subject of this discussion is not communication in general, but only the problem of receiving a revelation from God. It is frequently said by modern theologians that such a revelation is impossible. God is described as the "totally other," and incapable of being reached in any comprehensible way. Some prominent scholars have lately vied with one another in proclaiming that God is dead; that is, that the God-concept does not correspond to any objective reality, but only to the "ground of being" or to the highest human aspirations. Such views, of course, make any revelation from God to man impossible. The Bible may then be a revered book, or an heirloom treasured for its high ideals, but it cannot be a communication from God.

A true revelation is conceivable only to those who believe in a

living God. The taunt of the prophet Elijah challenged the
prophets of Baal: "Cry aloud; for he is a god: either he is
musing, or he is gone aside, or he is on a journey, or peradven-
ture he sleepeth and must be awaked" (I Kings 18:27). Elijah's
irony put in focus the real issue: obviously Baal was no god at
all. Were he a living deity, he could and would respond to the
importunity of his worshipers. By contrast, the Hebrew prophets affirmed their faith in a living God who could answer by fire.
The idols were nonentities. The Psalmist stated this contrast
graphically:

> Our God is in the heavens:
> He hath done whatsoever he pleased.
> Their idols are silver and gold,
> The work of men's hands.
> They have mouths, but they speak not;
> Eyes have they, but they see not;
> Feet have they, but they walk not;
> Neither speak they through their throat.
>
> (Psalm 115:3-5, 7b)

The positive aspect of this contrast is stated more fully elsewhere in the Psalms:

> He that planted the ear, shall he not hear?
> He that formed the eye, shall he not see?
>
> (Psalm 94:9)

God is greater than His creation. He is infinitely superior to men
in power and glory, but, as the Psalmist put it, He is in no wise
less than the creatures He has made. He cannot be less than
personal. To deny personality to God is to degrade Him, however the theory may be embellished by calling Him the Absolute,
the Infinite, the Totally Other, or the Ground of Being. Such conceptions of a god do not present a being who is the object of
love, and cannot allow a real revelation from God to man. Such
a god is no better than the idols of Jeremiah's day who were
fastened with nails and hammers and of necessity were carried
because they could not walk. "They cannot do evil," the prophet
says, "neither is it in them to do good" (Jeremiah 10:5).
    Some current opinion holds that new understanding of the
vastness of the universe has made it impossible to believe in a

real God: witness the Russian astronaut who after his first flight into space concluded that there was no God because he did not see one. He seemed not to suspect that he was looking in the wrong direction. But it is surely true that the denial of a real and living God involves the impossibility of any divine revelation. A dead God can do no miracle, speak no truth, issue no commands. One may speak of blind forces or inscrutable principles, but where there is no personal God the problem of communication finds no solution.

Many modern thinkers wishfully believe that they can stop here, but they cannot. The denial of a real God involves the alternative that absolute chance is deified. The universe becomes a meaningless jumble originating in an explosion and terminating in a burnt-out future with neither purpose nor goal. To maintain any meaning in life or any validity in thought in the midst of such a chaos is a feat too great for any philosophical gymnastics. Not only is the possibility of communication from God to man denied, but also the validity and meaningfulness of communication from man to man is destroyed. As a result artists of this persuasion now convey their thoughts by random splashes. Musicians compose their works by tossing a coin. A flood of cynical literature expresses a great malaise which is the necessary consequence of the hypothesis of the death of God.

Against such abject scepticism the Christian faith makes vigorous protest. First, one must observe that no man can live by such a creed. A man may claim to paint by chance, but he eats, works, and loves by choice and design. If he can paint only by splashes, why does he paint at all? His effort to express his sense of scepticism is itself a denial of his creed that all is purposelessness and accident. His sense of malaise, of *Angst* and *Sorge*, is an indication of the reality of a personality which his creed denies. He cannot lift himself by his bootstraps to find meaning in an allegedly meaningless world. Neither can he jump out of his skin and rest content to be a cipher when God has actually put eternity in his heart.[1]

By this one merely echoes the old theistic arguments. If there is no God, there is no basis for truth, goodness, beauty or meaning, and so existentialism and the new morality deny them. But since they cannot actually be denied in practice except by the mentally deranged, one must conclude that inherent in the universe there is a God who creates, who acts, and who also can communicate.

There is a parallel here to the historical argument. Much modern scepticism traces back to ideas such as those expressed by Lessing that the historical cannot be a revelation of the eternal. This, he said, was a deep ditch which he could not jump over. In other words, God cannot act or speak in history. Perhaps this might be called Lessing's Law! It is a widespread conviction, but has it any firm foundation? What basis does it have more than the *ipse dixit* of nineteenth century philosophers? Such a view obviously excludes miracles, because it assumes that historical phenomena are produced by principles that operate with unvarying uniformity. Science is essentially descriptive, and must assume basic uniformity if the universe is to be interpreted coherently. It is, however, one thing to assume the coherence of the universe, and quite another to assume that all the factors of the universe are within the ken of the scientist. A personal God cannot be limited by rules that an observer creates for him. If Deity exists, the rules are His to make and the scientist's to discover and formulate. Not true science but philosophical scientism denies the possibility of miracle. If miracles happened in the Bible records, Lessing's dilemma is spurious and philosophical scientism has erred.

Consider the converse of Lessing's principle. If miracles and revelation have occurred in history, then philosophical speculations cannot deny the existence of the transcendent personal God of Christian faith. This was the simple testimony of the man born blind: "One thing I know, that, whereas I was blind, now I see" (John 9:25). The fact of the resurrection of Christ was enough to enable the early Christians to withstand opposition. Paul's argument before Agrippa seems conclusive: "Why is it judged incredible with you, if God doth raise the dead?" (Acts 26:8). To deny the possibility of this miracle, says Paul, is to declare that there is no true living God. And although it can easily be observed that there is no god presently in orbit in the stratosphere, he is a bold man who would think he can demonstrate that no God exists. Without such an anti-theistic demonstration, the possibility of divine revelation cannot be denied.

The Basis of Communication

It is also essential to the Christian faith to hold that there is a certain congruity between the Revealer and the recipient of revelation. Men do not talk to oceans except in poetic apostrophe. It is probable that talking to animals should not be called communication, even though here also there is a modicum of congruity. A dog may respond obediently to a command, but is this any more than animal training such as may be done with rats by bells and electric shocks and food? Men do not really converse with dogs; they train them.

God is indeed vastly different from men, so much so that His nature is veiled in mystery and hid from sight. Nevertheless it is basic to the Christian position that God is in some measure like men because He has made man in His image. Observe that God can communicate not merely because He assumed human nature in the incarnation, for the purpose of the incarnation was not basically to communicate, but to redeem. Communication occurred before incarnation, indeed before sin entered into the world. God *is* in some measure like us.

The Greeks objected to this thought, believing it to be foolish. They said that if a triangle could talk, it would say, "God is a triangle." Perhaps the Greeks spoke better than they knew. If a triangle could talk, it might be correct in saying, "God is a triangle," for a triangle that could talk would no longer be a mere triangle, but would be a three-sided figure with rationality and personality. In this attribute lies the image of God. God is not six feet tall like man, nor three-sided like a triangle. God is a personality like man, though infinite in His being, wisdom, power, holiness, justice, goodness and truth. To say that God is anything less than personal, to think of Him as the Absolute or Totally Other without personality, does not exalt God, but degrades Him to the status of an idol less than man, a being one could neither love nor understand. God must be personal as well as infinite, or communication becomes impossible, creation becomes an accident, and providence becomes an illusion. The

Christian thankfully prays to a person, "Our *Father* who art in heaven."

If it is clearly understood that the Christian believes in an infinite personal God, and if it is clear that he believes that men are made in the image of God, then problems of communication fall into their rightful place and can be studied in detail. If God is God and man is human, then communication from God to man is quite possible, depending upon God's good pleasure and upon the human will to receive such a revelation as God may give. One should ever keep in mind that men can deny the possibility of revelation in the Christian sense only after they have proved that there is no God or that men are not made in His likeness. The first point could hardly be proved without an exhaustive knowledge of the physical and spiritual universe, and the second point could hardly be proved until God's own nature is fully known.

THE METHOD OF COMMUNICATION

There still remains the problem of the possibility of a method of communication. Perhaps the distance from the infinite God to man is so great that no communication is possible for Him. Perhaps also something has intervened in man's status before God so that He does not care to own men as His children. Perhaps they are such fallen creatures that all revelation must be an approximation, an impression, a blundering response to overtures divine. None of these things would rule out the possibility of revelation of some kind, but they would bring into question the Biblical revelation of Christian faith.

Probably it would be admitted in major currents of thought that if God has revealed Himself anywhere, He has spoken in the Bible. The competitors to the Scriptures are not very successful. The Koran is the product of an energetic but sensual mind; its descriptions of paradise border on lechery. Its history is probably so twisted as to confuse the period of Moses with the time of the Virgin Mary. The sacred scriptures of the East fare no better. The writings of Confucius are worthy and true in certain aspects — just as the multiplication tables are true — but Confucius does not offer any counsel as to what one should believe concerning God. The Buddhist and Hindu writings can be judged somewhat by the bondage of their devotees who regard the snakes and cows of India as too sacred to kill, and who massacre only fellow humans. To do more than to mention these matters would require studies such as are found in books on the religions of the world, but the conclusion may here be allowed that if God has spoken anywhere, He has done so in the Bible. The Bible itself insists that He is revealed also in His handiwork, but it may be questioned whether such a revelation may properly be called communication. More likely it should be classified as revelation to be understood by inductive study as one seeks to think God's thoughts after Him.

If the Bible be called a revelation, what sort of a revelation is it? It is written in human language. Given in Hebrew, Aramaic and Greek, it is composed of words in their appropriate syntactical units of phrases and larger groupings. Words, however, are approximate in meaning. One asks for coffee and the waitress asks if it should be "white or black"? Of course no coffee is white or black; it is brown. One may say the day is gloomy because the sun is under a cloud. Fortunately for us, the sun is actually over the cloud by millions of miles. Who could communicate accurately with such a language?

It is possible to think that words never express exact thoughts but always mean one thing to the speaker and a different thing to the hearer. For this reason exact sciences like mathematics substitute symbols for words and use them in equations. Physicists put the pressure-temperature-volume relation of gases into an equation: $v = T/P$. Unfortunately, if exactitude be required, the equations are recognized to be not absolutely accurate because this very law of Boyle and Charles is only approximate, and in any case volume, temperature, and pressure cannot be determined with infinite precision. Consequently symbols as well as words are approximate, and it may be doubted whether the new mathematical logic is entirely successful in attaining results by setting up mathematical relations. Symbols must be defined by words, and words do seem to be approximate. Is communication ultimately possible, therefore, even between man and man?

Others contend that words, if carefully chosen, are invariable in meaning. If language constitutes legal tender in the exchange of ideas, the verbal concepts must be stable, and words of common speech must have uniform meaning for all who use them. On the other hand, how should one interpret the question, "Did you ever see a horsefly?" The same combination of sounds and letters in "horsefly" might refer to an insect or to the action of a quadruped. Furthermore, words are continually changing meanings, with resultant misunderstanding between localities or generations. How would those who believe that expressions are invariable in meaning explain puns?

After perusing so many words in this book already, the reader cannot be totally sceptical as to their place in communication. Every translator knows that words have not one simple meaning, but usually an area of meaning. They may have a formal sense, a slang sense, a particular sense in certain phrases and a technical sense in the jargon of a special profession. When two people communicate they share these areas of meaning. The old oaken bucket may bring to mind a brick house to one man and a log cabin to another, but it is in any case a water pail. In their context words are definable within such narrow limits that, aside from blunders of writers and readers, they convey real ideas within acceptable limits of accuracy.

This is all that one can claim for God's revelation in the Bible. Warfield says of this doctrine that "the Spirit's superintendence extends to the choice of the words by the human authors (verbal inspiration), and preserves its product from everything inconsistent with a divine authorship — thus securing, among other things, that entire truthfulness which is everywhere presupposed in and asserted for the Scriptures by the Biblical writers (inerrancy)."[2] This doctrine does not say that every sentence is spoken with a precision sometimes not possible for our ideas, to say nothing of our words. God's purpose was evidently to convey ideas within acceptable limits of accuracy. At one place He might date an event as after six days; at another He says it was about eight days later. If the altar was made three cubits high, we need not worry about the allowed tolerances of measurement. Three cubits according to the practices of the time is intended and three is the proper figure given within acceptable limits of accuracy. These limits are to be kept in mind not only in numbers and measurement, but in all the ideas conveyed. Precision and accuracy are not terms exactly equivalent to truth. The fact that a word cannot be exhaustively and precisely defined does not mean that it cannot be used appropriately to convey an idea, otherwise one should never be able to order a meal in a restaurant.

To speak with some degree of approximation is yet to speak truly. The Bible speaks truly and conveys the ideas of God within normal limits of accuracy acceptable both to man and to God. The admitted inaccuracy of words in approximation is no bar to communication upon earth nor to communication from God to man, nor is it a violation of the doctrine of verbal inspiration as above defined by Warfield. It does doubtless necessitate further exegesis and the close study of strange words in old and foreign tongues, but this is an admitted responsibility and obviously allows a high degree of certainty in results. Protestants have emphasized the teaching of the perspicuity of Scripture. As the Westminster Confession puts it: "All things in Scripture are not alike plain in themselves, nor alike clear unto all; yet those things which are necessary to be known, believed, and observed, for salvation, are so clearly propounded and opened in some place of Scripture or other, that not only the learned, but the unlearned, in a due use of the ordinary means, may attain unto a sufficient understanding of them."[3] The epistles of Paul are not gibberish; God gave a reliable revelation. Just as men may know God truly though not comprehensively, so the words of the Bible reveal truth even though they do not speak with infinite precision.

Propositional Communication

It is claimed by neo-orthodoxy, and by other views as well, that the Bible is not now believable; its claims cannot be accepted by the twentieth-century man. Therefore, and in accordance with Lessing's dictum quoted above, he seeks for a mystical vertical communication, not the verbal communication of propositional revelation.

There are two things to consider here, the first of which entails long hours of patient Bible study. Is the Bible believable?

Does it falsify the records of the patriarchs in Canaan, or are they only legends after all? All savants of critical bent once agreed that the patriarchal stories were unbelievable. More recent archaeological study has convinced most scholars that these stories are quite true to the life and customs of their day. Only patient exegetical and archaeological study could decide this question. There is no inherent reason why these stories cannot be received, and they are easier to believe in the mid-twentieth century than formerly. But how about the endless "contradictions," the old "three-storied universe," evolution, the miracles? Again, these problems must be faced one by one. The author has considered a number of these objections elsewhere[4] and other books on such subjects are also available. The contradictions are usually imaginary or easily explainable. The "three-storied universe" is the result of poor exegesis of the text. As Deuteronomy 4:15-18 makes plain, the alleged three stories are simply the sky, the land and the seas. The so-called "waters under the earth" merely refer to the water of rivers, lakes and seas which are below shore line. This is plain because verse 18 refers to these waters as the abode of fish. Evolution is indeed a firmly entrenched theory, but it is apparently changing to a new variety sometimes called polyphyletic evolution, which holds that there were various evolutionary trees not related to one another. This form gives promise of being somewhat more reconcilable with the Biblical statements, though much study remains to be done. The matter of miracles is a philosophical problem. As mentioned earlier, Paul gave a highly satisfactory answer to that problem when he said before king Agrippa, "Why is it judged incredible with you, if God doth raise the dead?" (Acts 26:8). Miracles cannot be the product of human agency; they are evidence of supernatural intervention. If man could do miracles they would be no proof of God's activity. C. S. Lewis has treated this problem of miracles very adequately.[5]

Problems there are, but they are not insuperable. The answer to these problems depends heavily upon the attitude with which they are approached. If one approaches the Scriptures humbly, remembering that he lacks many of the details of ancient culture, history and language, the problems will usually be seen in a better light. If he imposes on the Biblical text expectations based on current practices and sceptical ideology, he will find the problems difficult. It is not a necessary conclusion that the Bible can no longer be believed by the twentieth-century man.

The second objection, that the Bible is not to be taken as propositional revelation, violates the consistent Biblical claim. The neo-orthodox slogan, "Truth is personal," is neither valid in human relations nor is it applicable to human communication. Such a revelation would not be an answer to man's deepest needs for a revelation from God. The simple fact is that men are not pure spirits, but are both soul and body. How communication may be maintained by the spirit when the body lies in the grave is unknown, but at present communication with other beings or with the world is through the senses. Place two people in a room shielded so they cannot see, hear, or touch each other and there is no communication. God may indeed by His Spirit directly plant in men's minds suggestions of which they are not aware, but these cannot be studied in detail. Again and again God verbalized His message to the prophets — often through a visual angelic appearance. The prophets and apostles claimed that they spoke propositional truth. We have no knowledge of truth that is personal but not propositional. Behaviorist linguists have gone so far as to say that thought is only silent verbalization. This view is extreme and cannot be supported, but it is equally difficult to support any concept of communication without involving the use of the senses. God's inspiration of the prophets was indeed mysterious, but the teaching of the Bible is that it was a conveying of truth communicable by the prophet in words. Jesus preached using words. His claim was, "The words that I have spoken unto you are spirit, and are life" (John 6:63).

One may grant that truth must become personal to be effective, but the slogan "Truth *is* personal" does not express the facts of experience nor the teachings of the Bible. It is an escape mechanism to satisfy the view that God communicates somehow, using a Bible that twentieth century man believes is not true. Possibly instead of trying to change the view of the Bible the problem should be answered by trying to change the twentieth-century man, just as the church has tried to change unbelieving man for nineteen centuries already!

All agree that truth to be effective must become personal. A purely intellectual knowledge of the truths of God has no saving efficacy. There is nothing new or startling in such a view which was put into words by James (2:19). Propositional revelation will not save a soul. Faith was defined by the reformers to include knowledge, assent and trust. Propositional revelation is a first step in the saving work. God has spoken; trust in His Word is the step that completes the relationship. Men hear, understand, agree; and then commit to God their lives and their eternal souls. To trust in the unknowable and to commit one's way to a great question mark is neither good psychology nor good religion. "How shall they believe in him whom they have not heard?" (Romans 10:14).

A propositional revelation from God is, therefore, real and essential. God has spoken by the prophets of old and now by His Son. Whether men will hear or forbear, God has spoken. The objective propositional revelation is a savor of life to some and of death to others. The word spoken by Jesus shall judge the unbeliever in the last day (John 12:48). God has given a factual communication which is true.

A striking confirmation of this position is to be seen in the Biblical view of prediction. The Bible insists that the prophets and apostles and Christ Himself predicted future events. Much ingenuity has been expended by hostile critics to rob these Scripture passages of their force. The prophets are post-dated to a period after the fulfillment of the events allegedly predicted. The Old Testament predictions concerning Christ are re-interpreted to refer to events contemporary with the prophets, which are only later applied to Christ. Christ's prediction of the overthrow of Jerusalem is declared not to be genuine. Again, there is no space to discuss these items in detail. The author has so treated the Messianic Psalms elsewhere[6] and many other studies are available. One's approach will be greatly influenced by his attitude. If God cannot speak, then prediction is impossible. By the same token, if prediction is real, then God has spoken and has done so in propositional revelation. This argument is drawn out at length in Isaiah 41-46. Several scattered verses such as 41:22, 42:9, 45:20, 21, declare that the God of Israel can predict the future in contradistinction to the idols of the heathen. A singular proof of the reality of this God of Israel is that He has foretold the coming of Cyrus (Isaiah 45:1-4; 41: 22-25, etc.). This is the very section of Isaiah which is now so often dated after Cyrus' coming. It would make the author of these chapters a cheat and a skillful liar who claimed to predict the future, but actually was writing past history. It is demanding a great deal of credulity to expect one to think that the author of Isaiah 40 to 46 was a cheat and a deceiver. Rather, the Bible is what it claims to be throughout, a real revelation from the living God in verbalized form.

FURTHER PROBLEMS OF COMMUNICATION

There are subordinate problems of communication yet to consider. Did God so control fallible men as to give through them a true revelation? Indeed, could He? There is only one proper answer to the question, "Can God?" and Jeremiah gave it long ago: "Behold I am Jehovah, the God of all flesh: is there anything too hard for me?" (Jeremiah 32:27). The God who made man's mouth and mind can use it in any way that He wishes. He could have given His revelation in many different ways. He actually has spoken audibly, spoken and appeared in dream or vision, and produced a powerful impression by His Spirit's secret work. How is this revelation communicated to others by the prophets, the recipients of revelation? The facts and teaching of Scripture make it plain that God used the prophets and apostles according to their own personalities. So Moses writes as a lawyer, David as a poet, Isaiah as an orator, John as a reflective thinker. Yet these men worked so under the control of the Spirit of God that they gave in human words under acceptable limits of accuracy of expression the very truth of God, inerrant in fact, doctrine, or judgment.

Many Scripture verses make this explicit claim. The clearest is probably Matthew 5:17, 18 where, in the Sermon on the Mount, Jesus says that the Old Testament is letter perfect. Perhaps the most remarkable is Luke 16:31 which says that the revelation of the Old Testament was more significant than a miraculous resurrection.[7] On almost all sides today it is agreed that Jesus believed the Old Testament to be true throughout. He was not a

destructive critic; He referred to the Old Testament as true in
its history as in its doctrine. He appealed to its prophecies as
predicting His own work. He quoted the creation story, mentioned
the Mosaic authorship of the Pentateuch, etc. For a Christian this
would seem to be enough. There are problems in the Old Testament, and for some few of them the answers may not be known.
He who knows all the answers assured us that the "scripture cannot be broken" (John 10:35). Furthermore, He promised the Spirit
to the apostles to remind them of the words He had spoken (John
14:26). So the apostles could call their writings Scripture as well
as the Old Testament, being communicated by the same Spirit (II
Peter 3:16; I Corinthians 14:37; Revelation 22:18, 19, and others).

THE PROBLEM OF PRESERVATION

There is a final problem for our view of God's communication
of His revelation to man, the problem of the preservation of the
message. Granted that the living and true God has spoken and
that human words present a medium of acceptable accuracy,
and granted also that God's Spirit is able to superintend the
verbalization of the message, what about the Bibles printed today? They obviously contain mistranslations and even minor
mistakes. Of what use is an inerrant original writing of prophet
or apostle, if no one has ever seen it and it is totally lost from
recovery? This is the problem of textual criticism.

Many careful and orthodox men, such as Tischendorf, Westcott and Hort, have labored in this field of textual criticism.
Others also worked in this field in the early history of the church.
Tradition says that Ezra, the "ready scribe in the law of Moses,"
also was thus occupied. It is not a new study, though its principles have been on more solid foundations since Tischendorf,
and now the Old Testament textual criticism can be based on
a much more firm footing since the discovery of the Dead Sea
Scrolls.

One point may be mentioned at once. Some ask what the
evidence is for an inspired original if no one has ever seen such.
Warfield[8] has stated a helpful principle. He points out that
the purpose of textual criticism is not only to restore as far as
possible the original text, but also to test the present texts to see

how close to the originals they are. Thus textual criticism is by
no means a problem for verbal inspiration, but a supplement to
it. It can be shown satisfactorily that the original inspired text
has been providentially preserved free from serious error through
careful copying by devoted men.

There is much information concerning how this copying was
done. Monks in medieval monasteries prepared beautifully dec-
orated copies on parchment. With reasonable care these can last
over a thousand years. The author has a page of such a hand-
written manuscript 700 years old which looks as if it were printed
only recently. Magnificent ancient Bibles in the British Museum
and the Vatican Library are in a good state of preservation after
1600 years. Other copies have perished through the ravages of
war and time, but still many remain. Recently the sands of
Egypt have yielded even earlier copies of New Testament books
from about A.D. 200 to 250. The Egyptian papyrus is more fragile,
but these copies preserve large portions of the New Testament
— Luke, John, Acts, much of the Pauline Epistles and Revelation.
The copies of I and II Peter and Jude come from a later date,
about A.D. 300.

What do these copies look like? They differ from the text of
the King James Version only in details. It may be said in general that these earliest manuscripts show a text practically the
same as that used in the American Revised Version, and the late
medieval manuscripts show a text practically the same as that
used in the King James Version. Anyone can therefore test for
himself approximately how much variation there is among these
manuscripts by comparing these two versions. There is one
fragment of John called the Rylands Papyrus dated about A.D.
125. It is extremely early, being written within thirty years of
the original copy or at least within thirty years of the death of the
Apostle John. A translation of it reads exactly like the American
Revised Version. These facts reinforce the famous dictum of
Westcott and Hort that not one-tenth of one per cent of the text
of the New Testament is in dispute, and none of this concerns
any doctrine of our faith. The providential preservation of the
New Testament text without significant variation is assured.

The Old Testament was written much earlier, of course, and

scholars had despaired of having any early manuscripts of its text. There was Jewish witness that the Hebrew scribes of the Middle Ages were extremely careful. There is also evidence that ancient scribes in Babylon copied secular documents with high fidelity. For example, the Code of Hammurabi is well preserved in late copies of 700 B.C. as shown by comparison with the original inscription of 1700 B.C. But the finding of actual ancient Biblical manuscripts was too much to expect. The discovery of the Dead Sea Scrolls, preserved in desert caves, some of them in pottery jars, was welcome confirmatory evidence for the Biblical text. Parts of all the Old Testament books were found except Esther, although some of the books are represented only by small fragments (e.g. only six lines of Chronicles). Many of the pieces date from about 150 B.C., though some may be dated from 200 B.C., and a few from even about 250 B.C. The complete scroll of Isaiah was found dating from about 150 B.C. It was apparently in continuous use for 200 years. It is only 200 more years from these early scrolls back to the days of Ezra, Nehemiah and Malachi.

The content of these ancient scrolls closely resembles the present Hebrew Bible. Although the analysis of these manuscripts will probably occupy many more years, it is likely that they will confirm the text of the Old Testament as the investigations of Westcott and Hort stabilized the text of the New Testament. Some of these scrolls read more like the Greek Septuagint translation than like the current Masoretic text. The Septuagint was largely used by the apostles, was quoted freely in the New Testament, and was preferred by the Christian church for the first three hundred years of its existence.

Actually the support of the Septuagint gives welcome light on several New Testament quotations of the Old Testament which did not agree with the present Hebrew text. It can now be said that there is valid support for the New Testament form of these quotations. The main lesson of the Dead Sea Scrolls is that the present Hebrew Bible can be demonstrated to be not significantly different from that which was used about 200 B.C., except in such things as spelling and small details. The Dead Sea Scrolls will indeed help to reconstruct an improved text of the

Old Testament in several passages. They will answer some old problems and raise a few new ones.

One interesting new point is the support they give to the Septuagint text of Jeremiah which omits perhaps one eighth of the verses found in the Hebrew. Close study of the Septuagint will show that some of these omissions are due to the Greek copyists whose eyes jumped from one line to another nearby that began with similar words. Most of the remaining omissions of the Greek text of Jeremiah concern sections or verses which occur twice in the Hebrew. There are several such parallel passages in Jeremiah, and it may be questioned whether the Hebrew or Greek has the original. It makes little difference in any case, since nothing of the original material has been lost. The general evidence is that there is no variation of consequence between the best and the poorest Old Testament text. The providential preservation of the text of the Old Testament without serious problems is thus assured as in the case of the New Testament.

CONCLUSION

In this review of the problems alleged against the Bible as a communication of divine revelation, it is apparent that the main problem is unbelief. There have always been many who refused to believe in the living and true God. For them genuine communication is ruled out by their disbelief. It is not the advance of science that has brought into question the possibility of communication from God to man so much as the creeping secularism and open atheism of our day.

An attempt has been made to accommodate the idea of God to modern secular thought. God is then pictured as an undefinable Force, a non-personal Something. Such a god could not communicate since he is really of less worth and moment than man himself. A living, loving, sentient soul is of more worth than matter or impersonal force.

The Bible is a revelation in words which in their grammatical relationships communicate ideas. Words are not always precise, but communication of truth occurs constantly in spite of lack of precision. Christ in speaking to the Father affirms, "Thy word is truth" (John 17:17).

Revelation is propositional, for the Bible is full of statements of fact. Jesus frequently approved and guaranteed the facts stated therein. "In my Father's house are many mansions" is a statement of fact. "If it were not so, I would have told you" (John 14:1) is a guarantee of truth. The predictions of the prophets are also propositional revelation. They are true, or else the authors of these books were charlatans of the worst sort, deceiving the people in their very religion. If these prophecies are true, then propositional revelation is real and the God of the Bible has communicated His nature and purposes in very fact.

Some may ask the question, "Are the alleged facts of the Bible in contradiction to other solid knowledge?" Exhaustive studies of so-called difficulties and alleged contradictions have been undertaken by many. At the conclusion of these investigations most of the "contradictions" and "errors" have shrunk to mere "problems." There remains nothing that a man of faith and wisdom cannot accept.

The present copies of the Bible admittedly are not a perfect communication from God. These copies have been made by generations of fallible men, who erred occasionally in their work. Nevertheless close study of the evidence of ancient texts supports the view that the present editions are remarkably accurate copies of the words God spoke to men.

As stated above, the main problem in receiving God's communication is the problem of unbelief. Unbelief in God is what may be expected from a man lost in the meaninglessness of life and the deceitfulness of sin. God saw man in this lost condition and did not leave him to perish in his misery. He could have abandoned mankind and given no communication at all. But God so loved the world that He sent His Son to pay the price of redemption and win men back to Himself. Such a God can and will communicate. Although problems in this process may be acknowledged, yet one can say with all possible confidence that God has communicated to us His Word and will for our redemption.

35568

ARE THE SCRIPTURES
INERRANT?

Edward J. Young

Lincoln Christian College

Edward J. Young

Edward J. Young was the late Professor of Old Testament at Westminster Theological Seminary, Philadelphia, Pennsylvania. He was the author of *Introduction to the Old Testament*, *Arabic for Beginners*, *Studies in Isaiah*, and a *Commentary on Isaiah* in the "New International Commentary on the Old Testament" of which he was the editor. He held the Ph.D. degree from Dropsie College for Hebrew and Cognate Learning.

Chapter V

ARE THE SCRIPTURES INERRANT?

To speak of the Scriptures as inerrant is to invite immediate criticism. Many scholars are willing to denominate the Bible as God's Word, and to assert their belief in its inspiration, even in its plenary inspiration. When, however, one insists that the Bible is inerrant, they refuse to agree. The word "inerrant" is a red flag to them, and they will have none of it. To insist upon the inerrancy of Scripture is apparently to become obscurantist and ultra-fundamentalistic. To stress the Bible's inerrancy, they say, is to lose all opportunity for successful "dialogue" with the scholarship of today. So the argument runs. Is it valid?

The derivation of the word "inerrant" is clear. *Errare* is the Latin infinitive which means "to wander," and the concept of erring implies a departing or going astray from the truth. The prefix *in* has a negative force, actually somewhat privative, and is used in Latin and English just as it is also used in Babylonian.[1] Thus, the word "inerrant" simply denotes the quality of freedom from error, and it is in this sense that the word is applied to the Holy Scriptures. The inerrancy of the Scriptures, then, implies their freedom from any error of doctrine, fact or ethic. To state the matter in a slightly different way, every assertion of the Bible is true, whether the Bible speaks of what to believe (doctrine), or how to live (ethics), or whether it recounts historical events. On whatever subject the Scripture speaks, it speaks the truth, and one may believe its utterances.

Many contend, however, that it is dangerous to assert that any writing is inerrant. Liability to error is so common, that to make such an assertion concerning the Bible seems to be rash. This objection, however, is founded on the assumption that the Scriptures are purely human. If the Bible is the Word of God, then it would follow that all which God has spoken is in accord with truth and fact.

In making this assertion, however, one must be on guard lest he make another serious error. The Bible alone must tell us in what sense it is free from error. No one has the warrant or right to impose upon Scripture his own standards as to what is error, and what is not. Only the Bible itself can decide the sense in which it is free of error.[2] It will be necessary therefore to give some attention to the consideration of alleged errors in the Bible.

THE IMPORTANCE OF THE PROBLEM

There is a reason why the Christian believer insists upon the Bible's inerrancy, for he realizes that if the Bible has failed him at one point, he cannot be certain that it will not fail him at other points. If, for example, the New Testament is mistaken in referring to passages in Isaiah 40-66 as the work of the prophet Isaiah, by what warrant may one say that it is not mistaken in what it asserts concerning Jesus Christ? That irrepressible question is the reason why the Christian believer insists upon maintaining belief in the inerrancy of Scripture.

This position has often been misrepresented and misunderstood. It is misunderstood, for example, in a recent book which deals with the question of the inspiration of the Bible.[3] In this work Professor Beegle speaks of the maxim, "False in one, false in all," as though a writing which may be shown to contain error at one point, must contain error everywhere.[4] This, however, is not the contention of evangelicals. The Bible believer does not maintain that if there is one error in Scripture, then all of Scripture must be erroneous. What he maintains is that if there is one error in Scripture, he cannot be sure that there are not more. If the Bible has once proved itself to be false, is there any guarantee that it will not err more than once?

This poses another question. If there actually are errors in Scripture, what is the standard by which one is to judge what these errors are? The question is sometimes treated as though there were no difficulty at all; one seems to suggest that a person can simply read through the Bible and make a list of all the errors that are supposed to be there. When he has done this, he may apparently discard the errors and concentrate upon the remainder of the Bible.

It goes without saying that the problem is not that simple. Once one admits that there are errors in the Bible, he is immediately faced with the question how to determine what those errors are. Only he who has never given much thought to this question will speak as though it were easily possible to discover them. If there are errors, there must be some standard by which they may be found, and those who affirm their presence have not yet produced any criterion for identifying them.

That the question, then, is important, will readily be seen. If one concedes that the statements of the Bible may be erroneous, the door has been opened to a host of difficulties and the authority of the Word of God has been undermined. If Scripture has faltered at one step, how does one know that it has not faltered at more than one step?

SCIENCE AND THE BIBLE

It is almost axiomatic today to assert that the light of unfolding science has cast serious doubt on some of the precise tenets of proclaimed theology. The situation is caused not so much by an attack of science upon the Bible as by the fact that the discoveries of science have caused men to adopt a different attitude toward Scripture. At one time perhaps men did speak of an attack of science upon Scripture, but today it is simply assumed that science has brought to the fore light which compels an abandonment of the position that the statements of the Bible can all be accepted at face value.[5] This appears to be the case in particular with respect to the first chapter of Genesis, and as a result attempts are made to engage in a discussion of the relation between science and Genesis One.

Some simply assert that the first chapter of the Bible is poetry, not to be taken at face value, and consequently maintain that there is no conflict at all between the Bible and science at this point.[6] Such a procedure involves bad exegesis, however, and cannot really be taken seriously.[7] Others think that the Hebrews could not express creation in ordinary didactic prose but were compelled to employ the concept of myth.[8] Hence, the first chapter of Genesis is said to represent the beliefs of the ancient Hebrews, after it had been demythologized. Sober exegesis, however, compels one to take the chapter at face value. It means what it says, and no amount of exegetical legerdemain can overcome that fact.[9] How then can the first chapter of the Bible be interpreted in the light of the so-called findings of science?

Before any satisfactory answer can be given, the question must be set in proper perspective. If the first chapter of Genesis is merely a human composition, produced in the community of Israel, then it is nothing more than a reflection of human opinions, and it does not matter in particular whether or not it conflicts with the discoveries of the scientists. If, on the other hand, it is the Word of God, it must, in the very nature of the case, inasmuch as no man can have been present at the creation, be a revelation from God. If it is a revelation from God, one may well ask in all seriousness whether it conflicts with God's revelation in the created universe.

Genesis One teaches that God is the Creator of all things. It is characterized by a vigorous and robust monotheism, for it presents the Almighty God as the sole Creator. On this point of absolute creation scientists are often quite silent. They speak much about the origin of the earth, the solar system and the universe, but they are non-committal when dealing with the question of the absolute beginning of all things. The Bible, however, in contrast speaks in loud and clear tones. This does no credit to the scientist who does not mention ultimate origin, for how can one adequately discuss the nature of things without considering the problem of their origin?[10] It will not do to assert that all things are millions or billions of years old. Merely adding figure upon figure and cipher upon cipher will not come to grips with the question that demands an answer; namely, "Who made these things?" Inasmuch as scientists have been so silent upon this fundamental question, one may well wonder whether they are really in a position to assert that God's revelation is in error. It would be legitimate to question whether or not their procedures of investigation have not been grounded upon premises and presuppositions which would either exclude God from the picture or would somehow drag Him down into His created universe. Have the dominant hypotheses of the scientists been based upon a theistic foundation or not? It would seem that all too often they have not been so grounded, and if that is the case, the only other point of reference for predication is the mind of man, a shaky foundation indeed. In its clear-cut declaration that God is the Creator of all things, the first chapter of Genesis asserts the truth with a clarity and definiteness of which one need not be ashamed.

Are there, however, actually errors of fact in this first chapter? There was a time when men asserted that the mention of light before the sun was an error. Everyone knows, so the argument ran, that light comes from the sun, and the mention of the sun's creation should have occurred before that of the creation of light. Today, however, this objection is losing its force, for it is perfectly clear that there can be light apart from the sun. There appears to be a theological reason for the mention of light in Genesis 1:3, since light is the foundation of all that follows. This does not necessarily mean that such light came to the earth apart from the sun, for the sun may well have had a history parallel with that of the earth. It may have existed in some unfinished form as did the earth also and have been a light-bearer before it was brought into the relationship to the earth established on the fourth day. If this were the case, the problem would disappear. It may also be noted that in the so-called account of creation in Babylonian literature light appears before the sun. The mention of light before the sun was no mistake of Moses; it was deliberate and purposive. He who would accuse the Bible of an error at this point would be rash indeed.[11]

As this first chapter progresses, however, there appears what must be called a geocentric emphasis. The heavenly bodies are made to serve the earth, and science has given a glimpse of the vastness of space. What can be said about this point? The emphasis of Genesis is indeed geocentric, but it is not out of accord with anything that scientists have discovered. The Bible does not assert that the earth is the physical center of the universe as is sometimes erroneously maintained. What it does assert is that the sun and moon serve the earth, which is true. Whatever other functions the sun and moon may have, they do, as a matter of fact, serve this earth. That is all that the Bible says, and it is in perfect accord with fact in its utterances at this point.

Man cannot speak otherwise than from a geocentric standpoint. The most advanced astronomer talks of outer space and of sending up an astronaut, and by so doing, he is expressing a geocentric standpoint. It is impossible to do otherwise, and to criticize the Bible as presenting a naive viewpoint when it so speaks is simply not to come to grips with reality.

Perhaps the most serious exception to the first chapter of Genesis is taken in its use of the phrase, "after its kind." This phrase very definitely rules out an evolution of man from a lower form of life and also from one form of lower life into something that is essentially different from itself. But is the Bible in error here? Is the evolution of the species a proved fact? Obviously it is not, and it only beclouds the issue to assume that evolution has been proved. That there are difficulties is not to be denied, but who is in the position of being able to declare the Scriptures in error at this particular point?[12]

Nor does the Bible speak of the age of the earth. Should it be true, after all, that the earth is millions of years old, that would not disprove the Bible, for the Bible nowhere declares what the age of the earth is. Perhaps the figures of chronology given in the margins of some printed Bibles have caused confusion and uncertainty at this point, but it should be noted that these figures are not the text of Scripture itself. On the question of the earth's age, the Bible is silent.[13]

Serious reflection enables one to assert that it is impossible to point to any statement in the first chapter of the Bible and to declare that that particular statement is in error. For that matter, no one is able to discover the presence of error in this chapter.

This is, indeed, remarkable in consideration of the age in which Genesis One was committed to writing.[14] From the Babylonians there has come a so-called "creation" account, and among other peoples of antiquity also documents purporting to deal with the origin of the world have come to light.[15] No one would take these seriously as documents to be believed. It would be impossible, for example, to discuss the relationship between the Babylonian document and modern science. The very fact that men today are willing to consider the relationship of Genesis to science is in itself evidence of the uniqueness of Genesis. There is ample justification for making the assertion that here is an account of creation which, in all of its mighty and powerful declarations, is void of error because Genesis One is a revelation from the Creator Himself. It is the Word of God.[16]

These observations concerning Genesis have been written merely by way of illustration. There is really no conflict between any of the statements of the Bible and the findings of scientists. This does not mean that there are no problems; nor does it mean that the answer to every difficulty is immediately apparent. It does mean, however, that there are no actual contradictions. It is incumbent upon those who contend for the presence of actual error in Scripture to prove their assertion. Merely to point out difficulties in the Bible will not suffice.[17]

The question of the relationship between science and the Bible may be viewed with respect to another problem, namely, the resurrection of Jesus Christ from the dead. According to the Bible God performed a mighty miracle when He raised His Son from the tomb. Modern scientists, however, for the most part, do not believe in miracles; hence some refuse to accept the plain statements of the Bible. As was the case with the first chapter of Genesis, so also with the resurrection of the Lord; attempts are made to avoid the difficulty of direct encounter with the supernatural. The accounts of the resurrection are asserted to be only the faith of the early church. Hence, one must distinguish between the actual Jesus of history and the Christ of faith. This theme appears with many variations, but these variations are not now the main concern.

The main concern is essentially whether the Bible in asserting the miracle of Christ's resurrection has committed a gross error. The correct answer to this question presupposes a basis of genuinely theistic premises. If one believes that the dead cannot and do not arise, he will maintain that the Bible is erroneous when it asserts that Christ arose. He should therefore be challenged and asked what warrant he has for maintaining that the dead do not and cannot rise. Objections against the Bible which are based upon faulty premises must be ruled out of the discussion. Let a man examine the presuppositions of his thinking, and if he bases his thought upon the right premises, namely, those of a genuine Christian theism, he will be in a position to declare whether or not the Bible has at this particular point committed an error. The reason for this is simply that God, the God of Scripture, is the ultimate point of reference; He alone gives meaning to all of life, for He is the Creator. Unless one thinks His thoughts after Him, he cannot have true meaning in his utterances.[18] How then shall one think God's thoughts after Him? He Himself has revealed His will in the Bible, and so it is the Bible which must be the guide for thought.[19] The Christian philosophy of life must be based upon and consonant with the statements of the Scripture. Approaching the question of the resurrection then as Christian theists, believers would assert that God did indeed perform a mighty miracle for the simple reason that He has so stated it in His Holy Word. No man is in a position to assert that these declarations of the New Testament are in error. With respect to the resurrection of the Lord the Bible is true to fact. Jesus did rise from the dead; in so asserting, the Bible is guilty of no scientific or historical mistake.

CHRONOLOGY AND INERRANCY

One point of view from which it is often asserted that the Bible is not accurate is that of chronology. As is well known, the chronology of the Bible, and, in particular, of the Old Testament, is extremely difficult. Perhaps this is partially due to the transmission of the text, but not entirely. It would also appear that less is known about chronology than could be wished. Furthermore, as it stands in the Old Testament, it seems almost impossible to work out a satisfactory solution to some of the problems raised by chronology. The consideration of one or two examples will at least serve to indicate the nature of some of the difficulties.[20]

At first sight it would seem that there is a flat contradiction between the first verse of Daniel and Jeremiah 25:1. Jeremiah speaks of the fourth year of Jehoiakim, whereas Daniel mentions the third year. Furthermore Jeremiah equates the fourth year of Jehoiakim with the first year of Nebuchadnezzar, whereas Daniel asserts that in Jehoiakim's third year Nebuchadnezzar the king came against Jerusalem and besieged it. In the light of these phenomena some commentators have not hesitated to declare that there is present an actual contradiction. How can one speak of the inerrancy of the Bible in the light of such a situation?

In dealing with such phenomena one must remember how little is really known concerning the chronology of antiquity. Factors may enter into the calculation which are still unknown. In thise case, however, there is a solution of the difficulty which has much to commend it. One cannot dogmatically assert that it is *the* solution, for such would not be the course of prudence. At least, however, it seems evident that there is no warrant for the assertion that an actual error of chronology is present in either Daniel or Jeremiah.

Apparently Jeremiah and Daniel were employing two different modes of reckoning. According to the Babylonian method, what would currently be regarded as the first year of reign was known as the year of accession to the throne. The second year was then considered as the first year, and so on. If this is the method employed in Daniel, then it is obvious that in making mention of the third year of Jehoiakim, Daniel has in mind what would be considered the fourth year. There is thus a correspondence and agreement between Daniel and Jeremiah. Jeremiah evidently employs at this point the Palestinian method of reckoning the king's years, whereas Daniel on the other hand uses the Babylonian method. The situation may be illustrated by means of a table.

DANIEL	JEREMIAH
Year of accession	First year
First year	Second year
Second year	Third year
Third year	Fourth year

If this be the answer to the problem it would appear that there is no conflict whatever.[21]

Not all cases of chronology, however, may be thus easily resolved. Isaiah 36:1 states, "In the fourteenth year of King Hezekiah, Sennacherib king of Assyria came up against all the fortified cities of Judah, and took them." In II Kings 18:13 the verse appears again. This simple and clear statement of Sennacherib's approach to the cities of Judah, however, is in reality a very difficult passage, and the difficulty is found in the numeral, "the fourteenth year." It is generally assumed that the campaign of the Assyrian king here mentioned occurred in the year 701 B.C., and if that were the case, then the accession of Hezekiah to the throne of Judah would have been in the year 715 B.C. Indeed, there are several scholars who believe that this is just what happened. Why may one not merely accept this year as the date of Hezekiah's accession? At first sight it would seem that there can be no objection to so doing, until it is noted that according to II Kings 18:1, 2 Hezekiah began to reign in the third year of Hoshea king of Israel and reigned for twenty-nine years in Jerusalem. The northern kingdom, however, fell to Shalmanezer in 721 B.C. (II Kings 18:9 ff.) and so Hezekiah must have begun his reign six years before Samaria's downfall, i.e., in 727 B.C. If the statements of II Kings 18:1, 2 are correct, therefore, Hezekiah cannot have begun his reign in 715 B.C. There is a further difficulty. Ahaz commenced his reign in Judah at the age of twenty (II Kings 16:1, 2), and continued upon the throne for sixteen years. This occurred in the seventeenth year of Pekah, who was followed in Israel by Hoshea who reigned for nine years (II Kings 17:1). Thus, Ahaz would have reigned for four years after the accession of Hoshea, or until three years before the attack of the Assyrians upon Samaria.

Various attempts have been made to solve the difficulty raised by the mention of the fourteenth year of Hezekiah in II Kings 18:13 and Isaiah 36:1. No lengthy discussion can be attempted here, but there is one possible solution for this seeming error of chronology in the Scriptures. Instead of reading "fourteenth" in the two passages adduced, one may simply read "twenty-fourth." Actually this would involve merely the substitution of one letter for another, thus changing *ESRM* (20) to *ESRH* (10).

In the original script in which the Hebrew was written these two letters are quite similar. Whereas they are easily distinguishable if clearly and carefully written, they are nevertheless sufficiently alike so that if one of them had been carelessly written the other might quite easily have been substituted for it. If this solution is to be adopted, it would seem to clear up most of the difficulties involved.[22]

At the same time one must note that there is no manuscript evidence in its favor. Even the recently discovered scroll of Isaiah from Qumran is in agreement with the traditional Hebrew text at this point. The substitution of H for M, therefore, if it really were made, must have taken place at a very early date indeed. Enough has been said, however, to show that one cannot assert positively that the Scriptures are here in error. Where there is the possibility of a reasonable solution of a difficulty there is no warrant for adopting a dogmatic attitude and for maintaining the presence of error.

It is only candid to acknowledge that there are some problems of chronology for which no apparent solution is immediately forthcoming. At the same time one is on safe ground when he asserts that no man today is in the position of being able to prove that the Scriptures are guilty of error in their chronology, when that chronology is properly understood.

Literary Characteristics and Inerrancy

Much has been written about the documentary theory of the Pentateuch. Into that question one cannot now enter, for it has been discussed many times, but it is necessary to speak briefly concerning the literary structure of the Bible. Two examples may be considered, both of which are in the forefront of present-day discussion.

In the first place there is the question of the relationship of the first two chapters of Genesis. According to the dominant critical school the first chapter of Genesis is the work of the priestly writer or school, whereas the second comes from the Yahwist. As far as chronology is concerned the first chapter is generally thought to be considerably later than the second. These two chapters, it is held, differ from one another in marked respects.

Their language is different; their thought forms differ, their conceptions of God, their general nature. Obviously, it is held, they are not the work of the same writer, and just as obviously, the Scripture is here a source of contradiction and error.[23]

This position that there are two conflicting accounts of the creation has become almost a dogma of negative criticism. It is nothing new but has been expressed in various "Introductions" to the Old Testament for years. It has been answered, strongly, firmly and decisively.[24] The Bible itself gives us the key to the solution, namely, the phrase which occurs in Genesis 2:4a, "These are the generations of the heavens and the earth." This phrase has been much discussed and much abused. In the recent Anchor Bible, for example, it is translated, "Such is the story of heaven and earth as they were created."[25] This translation, however, is incorrect, and must be rejected. The word here rendered "story" does not have that meaning. It refers rather to what has been generated or begotten or produced. Hence, to speak of the generations of the heaven and earth is to speak of what the heaven and earth have generated or produced. Thus, the following verses, namely, the second chapter, are not at all an additional account of the creation, but deal rather with what has come from heaven and earth. This phrase, "these are the generations," is a superscription and not a subscription. It introduces what is to follow and does not primarily serve as a conclusion to what has just preceded.

The first chapter of Genesis comprises the account of the creation of heaven and earth; the content of the second chapter is quite different. In this chapter Moses concentrates upon the creation of man as a preparation for the events of the temptation to be recorded in chapter three. Wholly different, therefore, are the scope and purpose of the two chapters.[26] For this reason there are apparent differences in the choice of vocabulary. The ideas of God, however, do not differ, although the style of the language does. Diversity of style is not necessarily an indication of diversity of authorship. A proper interpretation of these chapters shows that they belong together and complement one another. If the two chapters actually were from diverse authors and came from different periods in Israel's history, and if they actually were two conflicting accounts of creation, it is a psychologically strange fact that the editor of the book of Genesis should have placed them side by side at the beginning of the Bible. Such a blunder seems almost inconceivable when one considers the remarkable unity of composition and plan that appears in the book of Genesis. Considered merely from the literary standpoint, this work is that of a genius, and for such a genius to have been guilty of placing side by side two conflicting accounts of creation at the beginning of his work surpasses comprehension. There is an error here, not in the Bible, but in the judgment of the negative critics.

Another problem raised by literary criticism has to do with the relation of Isaiah 36-39 to II Kings 18:9—20:19. A mere glance at these two sections of the Old Testament will reveal that they are almost identical in language. According to the modern negative school of criticism, the chapters in Isaiah are later than those in Kings and the narrative in Kings is thought to be the original. It might be asked what difference it makes whether Kings or Isaiah be the original. The answer is that it makes a tremendous amount of difference. If the chapters in Kings arose previous to those in Isaiah, then it follows that the prophet Isaiah was not the author of the latter book. This creates almost insoluble problems for the question of the authorship of Isaiah. It creates far more problems, let it be said in passing, than it solves; indeed, it solves none.

Without entering into a thorough discussion of the question, the following points may be noted. The style of Isaiah 36-39 is prophetic and stands out in distinction from that of the remainder of the book of Kings. On the other hand, it fits in well with the style of the prophecy of Isaiah. Both chapters 36 and 37 of Isaiah have remarkable similarities particularly in the opening verses. In chapters 36-39 Isaiah the prophet is quite a prominent person. This is a striking point when one remembers how the writer of Kings treats the reign of Ahaz. In the discussion of this reign he does not mention Isaiah at all. Indeed, the writer of Kings on the whole has little to say about the individual prophets, and, apart from the treatment of Elijah and Elisha, deals with the individual prophets only incidentally. The prominence given to Isaiah in these particular chapters is unique, and contrary to the author's custom. This would seem to indicate that these sections were not an original, integral part of Kings. Second Chronicles 32:32 also states that Isaiah wrote the deeds of Hezekiah in his prophecy. Lastly, the presence in these chapters of the Isaianic expression, "the Holy One of Israel," is almost conclusive that they must have come from Isaiah himself. In addition, one should note that in Isaiah these chapters are rich in meaning and have a definite purpose, namely, that of joining together the two sections of the book. If they are original with the author of Kings, their purpose in the prophetic work is less easily explained.

The two examples in the realm of literary criticism which have just been considered make it clear that in the discussion of such questions a certain bias is often to be found. Adherence to a particular theory of the composition of the Biblical books often appears to be the guiding principle in one's advocacy of a certain position of literary criticism. To adhere to a theory is not in itself wrong, but it is wrong to adhere to a theory that would in effect countermand express statements or teachings of the Bible. When literary questions are considered from the standpoint of what the Bible actually teaches, one may see that at this point also the Bible is inerrant. It does not in any sense misrepresent the facts.

HISTORY AND INERRANCY

Are there not, however, errors of history and geography in the Bible? Such a charge is often made. In his little book, *The Old Testament as Word of God*, Dr. Sigmund Mowinckel has a list of supposed errors in the Bible. Among others he mentions the fact that the Bible claims that Shalmanezer took Samaria.[27] This, however, is said to be incorrect in that the capture of Samaria was due not to Shalmanezer but to Sargon. Mowinckel is not alone in this assertion, and, indeed, many serious students of the Old Testament have felt that there was here a serious inaccuracy. At first sight Sargon does speak in his inscription as though he had conquered the city.

It should be noted that the Bible does not state in so many words that Shalmanezer captured Samaria. Nevertheless, the implication of the Biblical language is that this was the case. The Scripture states (II Kings 17:5, 6): "Then the king of

Assyria came up throughout all the land, and went up to Samaria, and besieged it three years. In the ninth year of Hoshea the king of Assyria captured Samaria, and carried Israel away unto Assyria, and placed them in Halah, and on the Habor, the river of Gozan, and in the cities of the Medes." Although the text does not actually mention Shalmanezer by name, there would seem to be no doubt but that the king of Assyria, who in verse three of the same chapter is mentioned, is "Shalmanezer king of Assyria." Is the Scripture, however, in error in thus mentioning him, and was it actually Sargon who conquered the city?

At first glance it would seem unlikely that a book which is as accurate as is Kings would be guilty of such a blunder. A careful study of the annals of Sargon's reign has shown that this presumption is correct. Samaria apparently fell in the late summer or early autumn of 722 B.C., and Shalmanezer died shortly thereafter. At home there were difficulties and Sargon was faced with the task of securing his throne. In 720 he marched westward to quell uprisings in Syria and also in 720 he deported people from Samaria. Four years later (716 B.C.) he settled Arabian tribes in Samaria. Apparently Sargon's remarks do not deal with the conquest of Samaria in 722, but with a later time. If this is the case, it is apparent that Sargon is not the king of Assyria mentioned in the book of Kings. He may have been a general in the army of Shalmanezer, but he was not the king of Assyria referred to in the Bible.[28]

We are certainly far from saying that all the proper relationships of these events are as clear as might be desired, but at this point as always the Bible speaks with the voice of truth. It is the Word of God, and its declaration concerning the fall of Samaria can be trusted. It has committed no historical blunder.

One more point may be noted. Both Isaiah 37:9 and II Kings 19:9 mention Tirhakah, king of Ethiopia. Actually Tirhakah was not king at this time, but the mention is proleptic. More serious is the consideration that he was supposedly born in 710 B.C. and hence at this time (namely the year 701 B.C.) would have been only nine years of age and could hardly be called the king of Ethiopia, even if this were done proleptically.

Some scholars therefore have not hesitated to criticize the Bible and have assumed that the mention of Tirhakah is an anachronism. It is the part of wisdom, however, not to be dogmatic, and it is certainly not the part of wisdom to declare that Scripture is here guilty of an error. For one thing, the Egyptian chronology of this period is uncertain. Quite probably in the year 701 B.C. Tirhakah may have been twenty years of age, and if this is the case, the difficulty disappears. Some have sought to avoid the difficulty by the assertion that there may have been more than one Tirhakah. In the light of the prominence of the Ethiopian king, however, that seems to be a questionable procedure. The whole period is fraught with difficulty, largely because of our ignorance of the Egyptian chronology. Sufficient can be seen, however, to make it clear that the Bible in mentioning Tirhakah has not been proved guilty of committing an error.

THE BIBLE AND INERRANCY

Thus far this essay has simply sought to consider some of the charges which have been leveled against the Bible. The belief, however, that the Bible is the inerrant and infallible Word of God, does not depend upon human ability to show that the Bible is free from error. One does not believe that Scripture is God's Word on the basis of his ability to demonstrate that it does not contain errors.

The Bible is the Word of God because God has Himself so declared. If the Bible is the Word of God, then it is true and perfect, for it has been issued by the mouth of Him that cannot lie. The Word is the expression of His thought, and it is impossible that His thought be other than pure and holy. Hence it is that our Lord said, "The scripture cannot be broken." If there be errors in the Scripture, then the Scripture is broken. Furthermore, Christ gave the command to search the Scriptures, for they bear testimony of Him. His earthly life was lived in the atmosphere of the Old Testament, and all that transpired at the time of His sad arrest and betrayal was done in order that the Scriptures might be fulfilled.

The evidence that Jesus Christ believed the Scriptures to be the authoritative Word of God is rich indeed and has often been presented. It need not be repeated here. The assertion that there are errors in Scripture is a contradiction of Christ, for He held that view of the Bible which is today called orthodox; namely, that Scripture is the infallible, inerrant Word of the living God. If Scripture is not inerrant, then Jesus Christ was mistaken. It may not be popular to take a stand on the side of Jesus Christ and His apostles, but though it may not be popular, it surely is blessed, for our souls may then rest upon the truth of that holy Word of God, the Scriptures of the Old and New Testaments, which can never be broken.

THE INSPIRATION OF THE OLD TESTAMENT

Marten H. Woudstra

Marten H. Woudstra

Marten H. Woudstra is Professor of Old Testament in Calvin Theological Seminary. He was educated in the Netherlands, and studied theology at Kampen Theological Seminary. Later he continued his studies at Westminster Theological Seminary, from which he obtained the degree of Th.D. He was formerly pastor of the Third Christian Reformed Church of Edmonton, Alberta, and is the author of *The Ark of the Covenant from Conquest to Kingship* and numerous articles for periodicals and encyclopedias.

Chapter VI

THE INSPIRATION OF THE OLD TESTAMENT

BIBLICAL SCHOLARSHIP is presently flourishing as perhaps never before. Yet rarely has there been a time in which the Biblical doctrine of inspiration was under as severe attack as it is at the present. This confusing situation imposes upon the serious student of the Bible the obligation to take a new look at the pertinent Biblical data. Could it be that the traditional view concerning the inspiration of Scripture has not done justice to all the evidence? Since no human interpreter, however devout his commitment to Scripture, is immune from error, the question whether the traditional view of the inspiration of the Old Testament is defensible must periodically be faced.

A complete consideration of all the factors involved in the modern attack upon this doctrine cannot be expected within the scope of this essay. The basic question, which divides Biblical scholarship into two opposing camps, is in this area one of scientific methodology. To treat that question with any degree of thoroughness would require a hermeneutical rather than exegetico-systematic treatment. It is the latter rather than the former which is here presented.

In keeping with this purpose the ensuing discussion will center largely in an investigation of some of the Biblical data from the Old and New Testaments bearing on the doctrine of inspiration. The major part of this essay, found in the section "Is Inspiration a Jewish Concept?" has been devoted to that task. No exhaustive coverage is being attempted. By concentrating on some representative passages and by examining their bearing on the modern debate it is hoped that the general contours of the doctrine of inspiration will emerge.

In the meantime it will be necessary to set forth first of all the notion of inspiration as traditionally understood by evangelical scholars. In the second place, before coming to the Biblical evidence, the current state of Old Testament scholarship will be reviewed briefly as it pertains to the doctrine of inspiration.

THE MEANING OF INSPIRATION

The word "inspiration" may be used in at least two senses. The wider sense of the word applies to the general influence of the Spirit of God in the hearts of believers. Extending this wider use still further one may even speak of artistic inspiration. This general use of the word, however, should be carefully distinguished from the specific sense in which it is used in this essay. In this specific sense the word "inspiration" has a twofold aspect. It may refer to the *activity* of inspiration, or to the *result* of that activity. B. B. Warfield includes these two aspects in his description of inspiration when he states: "The Biblical writers are inspired as breathed into by the Holy Spirit so that the product of their activities transcends human powers and becomes Divinely authoritative."[1]

The same author continues to describe inspiration as "a supernatural influence exerted on the sacred writers by the Spirit of God, by virtue of which their writings are given Divine trustworthiness."[2] Thus for the purposes of this essay one may say that the inspiration of the Old Testament refers first of all to the divine activity which prevailed when the authors of the Old Testament books committed their thoughts to writing. In the second place it refers to the inspired quality of the Old Testament. Due to the inspiration in the *active* sense, the Old Testament now possesses divine authority and trustworthiness, which amounts to saying that it possesses inspiration in the *qualitative* sense.

Inspiration in the Context of Modern
Old Testament Scholarship

After thus delimiting the subject, the next step will be an examination of the context within which the present investigation of the inspiration of the Old Testament takes place. A consideration of this context becomes necessary in view of the fact that a contemporary statement of Biblical truth will then be relevant only if this statement is made with reference to the specific problems confronting Biblical scholarship at any given time in history. Failure to recognize this question of context would result in a corresponding failure to establish the doctrine of inspiration in such a manner that it could be grasped in terms of the contemporary problems.

During an earlier phase of Old Testament critical scholarship heavy emphasis was placed on the literary analysis of the supposed sources which were thought to underlie the Old Testament in its present form. These sources, especially those allegedly used for the composition of the Pentateuch and Joshua, were held to have been continuous documents before they were used in the composition of the Biblical writings.

While the adherents to the method of literary analysis were as a rule hostile to the traditional doctrine of inspiration, their method of investigation did not challenge this doctrine quite so directly as does the present phase of Old Testament criticism. Following the literary-historical method one may or may not adhere to the doctrine of inspiration. At least one may adhere to some form of that doctrine without directly coming into conflict with his method of study. But the contemporary emphasis in Old Testament scholarship has moved away from a mere literary analysis of supposedly written sources and documents. Today there is a far greater stress on the influence which oral tradition is supposed to have exercised upon the origin and composition of the Bible. Accompanying this stress on oral tradition is the notion that these oral traditions were decisively shaped by sociological processes which dictated as it were the very form and contents of a given bit of tradition-material. The term currently used to describe these communal sociological processes, which are thought to have had such a decisive role in the origin of the Biblical writings, is the German expression

Sitz im Leben. Literally this means "situation of life." Other terms by which the current phase of Old Testament criticism has been designated are: form-criticism, history of tradition, and *"Gattungsgeschichte"* (i.e., history of literary genres).

Spearheading this newer approach was the Old Testament scholar Herman Gunkel (1862-1932). Gunkel called attention to the manifold forms in which the ancient oriental oral and written tradition habitually expressed itself. This he did on the basis of a comparison of a variety of literary remains gathered from the literature of ancient civilizations.

Some of the results of Gunkel's form-critical methods relevant for the present investigation are: (1) A strong emphasis on the similarity of certain literary patterns observable both in the Old Testament and in the ancient Near East is developed; (2) the personal contribution of individual authors to their particular writing is minimized; (3) the form of a given Biblical utterance is viewed in close conjunction with its contents; (4) a consequent rapprochement has been established between the discipline of Introduction with that of "Biblical Theology"; (5) Biblical literature tends to be increasingly regarded as the product of an ever growing tradition. Within that tradition the substance of Old Testament teaching as well as the form into which this substance was poured are seen to represent certain fixed patterns characteristic not only of the Bible, but also of the literature of the ancient Near East in general.

Within this climate of scientific opinion the evangelical student of the Old Testament must reassert the doctrine of the divine inspiration of the Old Testament. It is a climate which leaves far less room for the traditional opinions regarding inspiration than did its literary-critical predecessor. If oral tradition played as large a role as current opinion asserts, and if this tradition already had a great deal of fixity prior to its inscripturation, where, then, does the doctrine of inspiration begin to be meaningful?

Or, to put things differently, if communal beliefs are as decisive in the shaping of the traditions as form-criticism asserts, is there any point where these beliefs begin to assume the form of divine revelation? Is not the interpreter's task completed when he has explained what used to be believed, whether this be *during* the tradition-process or *at the end* of it? Can a real doctrine of inspiration emerge from a form-critical method of interpretation?

The challenge which comes to the evangelical Old Testament scholar by means of this modern critical approach is great indeed, for he is confronted with a highly subjectivized type of "understanding" of the Biblical message which yet falls short of a complete understanding in terms of a divinely authoritative message. For this reason the orthodox Bible student does well to recognize that the most exhaustive treatment of Biblical proof-texts of the doctrine of revelation will not be sufficient as an argument in the current debate, unless first the question of hermeneutical method is faced and solved in a manner consistent with the total claims of the Bible. This concerns far more than what is usually understood by Biblical studies only. The destructive views of the modern higher critical approaches to the Old Testament can only be challenged by a concerted effort on the part of all branches of consistently Christian scholarship. When such an effort is not made, Biblical scholarship is bound to drift farther and farther away from its truly Biblical moorings. While offering fascinating bits of insights into what the Bible meant in terms of its own contemporary culture and custom, Biblical scholarship will be less and less able to state what the permanently valid and divinely authoritative meaning of the Bible is for all times and for all conditions of men.

Since a further pursuit of these hermeneutical questions would exceed the scope of this essay, merely calling attention to them will have to suffice at this point.

The Biblical Evidence for Inspiration

Some New Testament Passages

Though the evidence of the Old Testament with respect to its own inspiration is by no means wanting, the first procedure will be to survey some of the New Testament data. Examination of some Old Testament materials will be concluded with further evidence from the New Testament.

The New Testament witnesses to the inspiration of the Old Testament both explicitly and implicitly. Among the best known

of the passages belonging to the first category are II Timothy
3:16 and II Peter 1:21 which will be mentioned briefly at a
later point in this discussion.

Initial consideration will be given to the examination of a
group of passages which, while not asserting the doctrine of
inspiration explicitly, nevertheless bear witness to this doctrine
in less direct fashion. It is precisely the indirectness of the witness borne by these passages which may serve to make them
valuable.

The passages here referred to are those in which a New
Testament author or speaker makes a reference or an allusion
to an Old Testament passage. The precise point of interest in
this connection is the formula which is used when the Old
Testament material is introduced to a New Testament audience
or circle of readers. Thus Acts 1:16 represents Peter as saying,
"It was needful that the scripture should be fulfilled, which
the Holy Spirit spake before by the mouth of David concerning
Judas." Matthew likewise, in chapter 1:22, introduces the words
from Isaiah 7:14 to his readers in the following manner: "that
it might be fulfilled which was spoken by the Lord through the
prophet."

Matthew's introductory formula points to the high esteem he
holds for the Old Testament Scriptures. Though no longer having
direct access to that "which was spoken by the Lord through
the prophet" as did the Old Testament prophet himself, Matthew
nevertheless confidently asserts that the words which he is about
to repeat are in no way less that which was spoken by the Lord
than the original words themselves. The conclusion appears
warranted that the inscripturation of this prophetic word in
Matthew's estimation did not detract in the least from its being
the Lord's speaking through the prophet.

A passage such as this, while not asserting anything explicit
concerning the inspiration of the Old Testament in the active
sense of that word, does have significant implications for the
understanding of inspiration in the qualitative sense. Inspiration, as was noted earlier, results in the divine trustworthiness
and authority of the product of inspiration. To this divine trustworthiness of the written record the passage from Matthew and
other New Testament writers testify loudly. At the same time, it

would seem inevitable to conclude that the confidence with which Matthew identifies his written source with that "which was spoken by the Lord" is based on only one conviction. This conviction is that an act of inspiration in the active sense had endowed his source with the authority which was attributed to it.

The question now arises concerning the compelling nature of this kind of New Testament evidence. What does modern Biblical scholarship do with a passage like this? Is it ready to accept this evidence at face value? There is a certain sense in which this evidence is indeed accepted by modern Biblical scholarship, but this acceptance is not more than historical. All that is admitted on the basis of this kind of evidence is that, apparently in the circles of tradition in which Matthew moved and for whom he wrote, the Old Testament was regarded as divinely authoritative and inspired. Having drawn this "historical" conclusion Biblical scholarship then sets out to "interpret" how this view came to be held by Matthew and other "early Christians"! Some point to Jewish influences. Others have tried to reconstruct a so-called Testimonia Book which is believed to have been in existence at that time, and which is supposed to have furnished the Biblical authors with a fairly universally accepted set of Messianic passages from which they could quote. Still others point out that Matthew's view of the Old Testament was a typical product of his own time, that it was limited to his own insights, and hence not binding on the modern scholar who presumably uses much more refined methods of exegesis than did Christ and the "early Christians."

This, then, is the highly celebrated "historical" approach to questions such as this. How valid is this approach? Does being orthodox prevent one from taking seriously the historical circumstances under which the Bible was written? Does it mean that exegetical methods can never advance beyond what the Biblical authors did with the Scriptures? In the present writer's opinion, it would be a mistake to believe that the evangelists and other New Testament agents of revelation were Biblical scholars in the modern sense of that word. But this does not mean that one may now place a question mark behind their view of Scripture as no longer relevant or authoritative for a modern approach to the sacred text. It is true that they did not write with the same scientific precision as is presently demanded. Yet one's faith in the authority of Scripture cannot be maintained when the question of the correctness of their view of Scripture should become a matter of historical evidence only.

Unfortunately much of what currently passes under the name of scientific exegesis fails to take seriously the claims which Scripture makes for itself. Suppose that Matthew's view of the Old Testament were correct. Suppose that this view were more than the mere result of Matthew's particular *Sitz im Leben*. Would it not be methodological suicide to ignore this claim or to treat it as no more than a bit of interesting though in no way compelling "evidence"? Biblical scholarship frequently boasts that it has developed an objective method of evaluating the data. But is it really objective to hold to a view of historical evidence which robs the Biblical claims of their divinely compelling character? And can a truly Biblical theology be built on bits of this kind of historical evidence? This is the question concerning which Biblical scholarship is at present badly divided.

Some Old Testament Passages

Although the foregoing discussion does not exhaust the New Testament evidence or even begin to do so, attention must now be given to certain passages from the Old Testament. There will be a later opportunity to return to the New Testament materials.

One of the most significant phrases to be considered at this point is the expression "The word of the Lord" (Hebrew: *debar yahweh*), used to introduce some of the written prophecies of the Old Testament. This expression occurs frequently when the prophet describes a communication received from God. Each individual communication is described as "the word of the Lord which came." The use of this expression is not limited to individual communications. A number of prophetic messages combined into a book may also be so designated (cf. Hosea 1:1; Joel 1:1; Micah 1:1; Zephaniah 1:1). Hosea's ministry extends over the successive reigns of several Israelite kings, yet the entire message of his book is called "the word of Yahweh."

What, precisely, is the relevance of this for the doctrine of inspiration? There is a tendency in modern Biblical scholarship to deny that this usage has any legitimate bearing on the question whether books such as Hosea, Joel, etc., were inspired. Though Biblical scholarship admits that the doctrine of inspiration was subsequently deduced from the usage here discussed, it is held that such a deduction is not in keeping with the original intent of the expression.

To examine this contention in the light of the evidence, one must first seek to establish the exact force of the expression, "the word of the Lord." Subsequently an attempt will be made to assess the meaning of this phrase when used as a heading over some of the prophetic books.

Attention should first be called to the fact that the Hebrew *dābār* (word) possesses a good deal of force. It is highly dynamic in character. Jeremiah experiences this "word" as a fire shut up in his bones (Jeremiah 20:9) or as a hammer that breaks the rock in pieces (23:29; cf. 5:14). Modern theology has gone to excess in its emphasis on the dynamic character of the word, as has been correctly pointed out in James Barr's stimulating study, *Semantics of Biblical Language*.[3] Yet it is well to keep in mind that words in the ancient Near East in general, and in the Bible in particular, are regarded as more than mere vocables. While the Old Testament shares a certain affinity with the thought-world of the ancient Near East in this respect, it shows also an essential difference. Within the culture of the ancient Near East the power of the word was associated with magical practices of incantation and divination. That culture was dynamistic in character; that is, it believed in the existence of an impersonal power which by the correct manipulation of words could be used to the advantage or disadvantage of individuals or nations. Curses and blessings were potent because they were thought to have access to this impersonal power, directing it to the benefit or detriment of those blessed and cursed.

This is not the case in the Old Testament. It too believes in the power of the "word," but this power is not conceived magically. Yahweh is the only one who truly speaks a power-laden word. He speaks and it is; He commands and it stands. The power of the "word" in the Old Testament, then, is related to and derives from the power of Yahweh's Word.

It is against this background that the use of the expression, "the word of the Lord," as a heading of written prophecy should be appreciated. It is widely held in circles of Biblical criticism that the dynamic "word" suffers a degree of fossilization when used for written prophecy, but a closer look at the Biblical data does not bear out this contention. Jeremiah, as noted earlier, is fully aware of the highly powerful effect of the "word." Yet it is this same prophet who gives us an elaborate account of how this powerful instrument of Yahweh may be channeled into written form without loss of immediacy or directness. Yahweh's words are to be recorded in the "roll of a book" (Jeremiah 36:2). The purpose of this writing down of the words of Yahweh is to cause Israel and Judah to return from their evil ways (verse 3). The written words, therefore, are meant to be a no less powerful instrument for conversion than was the original spoken word. In terms of the qualitative meaning of the word "inspiration," as developed above, it follows that the written word in Jeremiah's case is fully as inspired as was the original oral communication.

This is also the inference to be drawn from the use of the expression, "the word of the Lord," as the heading of prophetic books. It has been suggested by Biblical scholarship that this inference, though made subsequently, was not in the original intent of the authors themselves. The Biblical authors, so it is argued, had too dynamic a view of the "word" to permit its extension to written books in their entirety. Only a later generation, holding to a more bookish view of inspiration, could have made this inference, so the contention goes. Before examining this contention more closely, another bit of evidence, also taken from Jeremiah's writings, should be mentioned. This concerns the letter written by Jeremiah to the captives in Babylon, as recorded in chapter 29 of his prophecy. Throughout this entire chapter Jeremiah purposely identifies his written message with the word of Jahweh (cf. verses 4, 8, 14, 16, 17, 20). The same may be said of the concluding part of the chapter where a separate communication receives a similar treatment (verse 30 ff.).

It would seem, therefore, that the Biblical evidence examined thus far clearly indicates that written words are to be regarded as fully adequate vehicles of God's thoughts, in no way less direct in either power or authority than their oral counterparts.

Should one not conclude from this that the writing process which produced this written and authoritative "word of Yahweh" was accompanied by a special divine influence which is called inspiration? How else could the human authors equate their written product with the very "word of Yahweh"? Did not these human authors know of the limitations of their memory to which they were naturally subject? Were they not aware of occasional errors in judgment and of a proneness to misrepresent events? How, then, could they be so bold as to attribute the quality of the "word of Yahweh" to the products of their pen? How could they identify these written products with these other communications directly received from God and likewise called "the word of Yahweh"? While presumably fully conscious of their own human fallibilities and knowing themselves to be men of their own times, they nevertheless confidently asserted that the product of their writing activity was indeed the very "word of Yahweh" itself.

The critical questions raised earlier still require some further scrutiny. Why, it is asked, does not all written prophecy bear the superscription, "the word of the Lord which came," etc.? Some prophetic books are introduced with formulas such as "the words of . . ." followed by the name of the prophet whose book it is (cf. Amos 1:1; Jeremiah 1:1). Does this variation in usage support the critical contention that the original authors of the prophetic books were not yet wholly committed to a bookish view of inspiration? Is there possibly an intermediate stage of development? Was there a hesitancy to extend the expression "the word of Yahweh" to written prophecies in their entirety, and is there any evidence that this expression was at first limited to those parts of the written prophecy which contained the specific communications of Yahweh? Was it left to a later, less "dynamic" inspiration belief, to draw the fatal consequence from all this?

A further consideration of these questions in the light of the evidence found in the book of Jeremiah may be helpful. This book, as was noted, does not bear the superscription, "the word of Yahweh." Nevertheless the absence of this superscription must not be interpreted as due to a certain hesitancy to use this expression for a book as large as that of Jeremiah. Th. C.

Vriezen contends that the probable reason why the heading "word of Yahweh" was not chosen for the great prophetic collections, such as Isaiah, Jeremiah and Ezekiel, was "because it was felt that these collections contained many other things besides divine messages."[4] If this is so, how then does one account for the fact that within the book of Jeremiah the expression "the word of Yahweh" occurs in much the same way as it does in the heading over some of the smaller prophecies? Chapter 32 may serve as an illustration. This chapter bears as its heading the customary phrase, "the word of Yahweh" (verse 1). Yet the rest of the chapter does in no way contain exclusively "divine messages" in the sense in which this is meant by Vriezen. The first "divine message" in the specific sense of the word does not occur until verse 6. Moreover, the greater part of this chapter is made up of materials which do not qualify when judged by Vriezen's criterion of "divine messages." Yet the chapter in its entirety bears the heading used for some of the prophetic books elsewhere. Does not this upset Vriezen's earlier contention?

Moreover, a further examination of Jeremiah's prophecies clearly demonstrates that the prophet shows no hesitancy whatever in identifying his words with the divine Word. In fact, at many points in this prophetic book one is at a loss to make a clear distinction between that which is more particularly the prophet's utterance and that which presents Yahweh as the spokesman. There is a blending of these two into one continuous discourse. In Jeremiah 8:13 Yahweh appears to be the speaker, yet in the next verse Jeremiah and the people seem to be speaking, while in verse 17 Yahweh is speaking again. From 8:18 through 9:6 the lines of demarcation are extremely dim. Some parts are said to be Yahweh's words (9:3 and 6). The rest of this lament is probably as much Yahweh's own lament for His people as it is Jeremiah's. In the light of this blending of the divine and the human, Vriezen's singling out of "divine messages" does not seem feasible. Of all the prophets Jeremiah would appear to be the least likely to have a hesitancy in identifying his written utterances with the word of Yahweh. Did not he describe himself as being "full of the wrath of Jehovah" (Jeremiah 6:11)? One may also compare the apparent

ease with which Jeremiah uses the expressions "words of Yahweh" and "words of Jeremiah" interchangeably (36:6, 10).

In the light of the foregoing discussion it appears warranted
to conclude that the use of the expression "the word of Yahweh"
in the heading of certain written prophecies presents a stupen-
dous claim. This claim can truly be maintained only if behind
it lies the conviction that during the writing process of these
prophecies nothing occurred that impaired the divine quality
and authenticity of the written message. Positively, it means
that a special influence, such as is meant in the traditional
doctrine of inspiration, directed the writers during their writing
activity and that this influence justified them in making these
claims.

Some Passages Dealing With Writing

Some attention should now be given to those Old Testament
passages which describe the process of committing to writing
certain matters for later consideration. Reference has already
been made to some of these passages, such as Jeremiah 36.
Certainly the most notable instance of writing activity in the
Old Testament is that attributed to God Himself, who with
His own finger wrote the "ten words" upon tablets of stone
(Exodus 31:18; Deuteronomy 4:13; 5:22; 9:10; 10:2, 4). The
very frequency with which reference is made to this in the
Pentateuch is itself of great interest. These "ten words," though
originally pronounced orally and under the most awe-inspiring
circumstances, had become part of an inscripturated document.
Yet they did not thereby cease to be what they were originally.
Though obviously this is not a case of inspiration as such, it
nevertheless exemplifies a truth which, as was seen earlier, is of
the greatest importance for a correct understanding of inspiration.

Other significant passages in this connection are those in which
Moses is said to have written down various matters. The things
written are described by phrases such as "law," "the words of
the covenant," and other terms (Exodus 24:4; 34:27; Deuteronomy 31:9, 24). Again one is struck by the close identification
of the words written with the "word of Yahweh." Deuteronomy
30:11, when compared with verse 14, teaches that the written

"commandments and statutes" are to be regarded as the "word." Of this "word" it is said that it is "nigh" unto Israel. Though written in a book it is also in Israel's mouth and heart, given designedly that Israel may do it (cf. Jeremiah 36:2, 3).

The general aim of Biblical writing appears to be that the thoughts inscripturated may be perpetuated. This is also the reason why writing and teaching go hand in hand (cf. Deuteronomy 31:22). The writing down of Moses' song is intended to make it Yahweh's witness (verse 21). The things which Israel must be taught are the ordinances and the law of Yahweh (Leviticus 10:11; Deuteronomy 31:11), but the instrument of teaching this law is the written document which can be read before the assembled multitude. The ultimate purpose of this learning process is that the people may know Yahweh Himself (Jeremiah 31:34).

Mention has already been made of the witnessing function of certain written documents (Deuteronomy 31:21). The word "witness," or "testimony," holds a central place in the Old Testament covenant arrangement. Some of Israel's most prominent cult objects, such as the ark, the tabernacle, and the tables of the law, have the word "testimony" attached to them. The fact that the same witnessing function is also ascribed to the written form of the song of Moses points to the dignity which is accorded to written documents, a dignity which approximates that of the ark and of the law tablets.

THE ATTITUDE OF CHRIST AND THE APOSTLES

Following this survey of some of the Old Testament data concerning its inspiration, consideration should be given to further evidence from the pages of the New Testament. From the abundance of material which could be discussed if space permitted only a small selection will be made.

The Words of Christ

The words of Christ as reported to us in the Gospels bear witness to the high esteem in which He held the Scriptures of the Old Testament. These Scriptures were for Him the authoritative means whereby disputes must be settled (John 10:35).

Jesus' appeal to Scripture, though formally perhaps similar to that of His opponents, the Jewish leaders, was materially different from that of the Pharisees and the scribes. The latter made void the word of God by their tradition (Matthew 15:6). Jesus did not practice a merely formal adherence to Scripture, yet He esteemed it as the very Word of God to man. In one of the Synoptic Gospels (Matthew 22:31), Jesus introduces an Old Testament quotation by asking the Sadducees whether they have not read that which was spoken unto them by God. Though the other Synoptic Gospels present a slightly different formula, the Matthean version of this event suggests how closely Jesus associated the written word with the Word of God spoken. Through the medium of Scripture the words of God originally spoken to Moses under the solemn circumstances of the burning bush are also spoken to the Sadducees.

The Attitude of Christ

Christ asserted that the Scriptures pointed decisively to Him. This accounts for the repeated references to what He "ought" to do. There was a compelling necessity behind His Messianic labors. This necessity was embodied in the prophetic claims made by the Old Testament (Luke 24:25 f.; 44 ff.). Christ regarded the Scriptures as a unity. Even a quotation from one single author may therefore be introduced as coming from "the Scriptures" (Matthew 21:42; 22:29; 26:56). Christ also emphatically stated that the Scriptures testify of Him (John 5:39). Worthy of note is also the manner in which Christ combined more than one prophetic passage, referring to them jointly as having been spoken by "the prophets" (John 6:45). This shows that in Jesus' opinion the various parts of Scripture as well as the whole of it formed one unbreakable unity.

The Attitude of The Apostles

The same esteem for the Scriptures is also evident in the words and writings of the apostles. Paul asserts that all that was written aforetime was written for our learning ("instruction," Romans 15:4). The function of Scripture as the instrument of learning to know God and His will is again clearly stated. This is essentially an Old Testament emphasis.

Some of the more central passages asserting the inspiration of the Old Testament have already been mentioned. Second Timothy 3:16 and II Peter 1:20, 21 are perhaps the most explicit in their assertion that the writers of the Old Testament were subject to a special divine influence which we call inspiration. The very explicitness with which these passages speak and the fact that many excellent treatises have been made of them would seem to render further discussion superfluous.

Of considerable interest for the doctrine of inspiration is also Peter's testimony in I Peter 1:10, 11. Peter affirms that the Spirit of Christ in the prophets made them prophesy of the suffering of Christ and the glory that should follow. The reader is also informed that the prophets themselves were not always completely aware of the full scope of their own words. Hence the prophets are represented as making diligent inquiry regarding the true implications of their prophecies. A probable example of this is afforded in Daniel 9:1 ff. Daniel appears to have been prompted to his inquiry by that which previous prophecy had recorded in written form. In the light of this Old Testament passage Peter's remarks about the prophets' diligent search assumes an independent significance as bearing indirect testimony to the doctrine of prophetic inspiration.

The cumulative weight of the evidence surveyed thus far points strongly in the direction of the traditional doctrine of inspiration as defined in the opening part of this essay. A final question must yet be faced which is prompted by a remark in B. B. Warfield's study mentioned previously, and which one encounters in contemporary writing as well. This problem concerns the question whether in its attitude to the Old Testament Scripture the New Testament followed an essentially Jewish approach. To the consideration of this question the final part of this essay will be devoted.

Is Inspiration a Jewish Concept?

The discussion of this question will largely concern terminological matters. In the present climate of ecumenical dialogue, however, the use of clear and unambiguous terms has become a prime prerequisite.

In his investigation of the terms "Scripture" and "Scriptures" as employed in the New Testament, Warfield observes that the use of this language in the New Testament "was an inheritance, not an invention."[5] He furthermore observes that "there was nothing left for Christianity to invent here" and that "the New Testament evinces itself in this matter at least a thoroughly Jewish book."

Within the context of Warfield's writings this utterance can be readily understood and appreciated, but within the context of modern ecumenical debate it is in need of further elucidation. There are those today who hold that the orthodox Christian concept of inspiration and of canon is an intrinsically Jewish concept. For this reason it is considered to be unworthy of an enlightened Christian position. There are others, however, who seize every opportunity to point out the "indebtedness" of Christianity to "Judaism." This is an attempt to do justice to the vital connection between the Old and the New Testament, but it has substituted the concept "Judaism" for the Old Testament. The two are not the same. This modern trend in the so-called Jewish-Christian dialogue is the approach of comparative religion masquerading under the guise of the ancient Christian affirmation of the vital continuity and unity of the two Testaments.

Had Warfield written with a view to the present situation with its almost universal surrender to the principles of comparative religion, he might have expressed himself more cautiously than he did. He might have clarified his statement about the New Testament in its use of the term "Scripture" being "in this matter at least" a thoroughly Jewish book. He might have pointed out more clearly that, as he himself would probably be the first to recognize, the Judaism of the early Christian period had already developed a distorted view of Scripture. He might have emphasized that the Christian church did not "take over" a Jewish canon as is sometimes alleged. The Christian church did not "take over" anything; it came into being as the ripe fruit of all that the prophets had spoken, culminating in the supreme embodiment of Scripture, Jesus Christ, the incarnate Son of God.

While the "indebtedness" of the Christian Church to Judaism may and must be stressed, every care should be taken not to use the word "Judaism" in the sense of comparative religion as is presently customary. The only Judaism to which Christianity owes anything is that which represented the pre-Pentecostal phase of the people of God under the old dispensation. Any other indebtedness of Christianity to Judaism does not concern essentials; at best it concerns peripheral matters.

Within the present ecumenical climate there appears a great need to stress once again the fact that Christianity does not owe its origin to Judaism plus the Christ-event. Christianity owes its origin to the Old Testament and to the Christ who came to fulfill that Old Testament because He "ought" (Luke 24:26).

This treatise has been offered in an attempt to set forth the doctrine of the inspiration of the Old Testament in the context of modern debate and denial. This doctrine is eminently scriptural. Its modern denials do not have the support of Scripture. Christians may continue to regard the Old Testament as they have always done; namely, as the very Word of God written.

THE INSPIRATION OF THE
NEW TESTAMENT

Clark H. Pinnock

Clark H. Pinnock

Clark H. Pinnock is Assistant Professor of Theology in the New Orleans Baptist Theological Seminary, teaching in the area of Systematic Theology and Apologetics, and was formerly Assistant Lecturer in the Department of Biblical Criticism and Exegesis, University of Manchester, England. He holds a Ph.D. degree in New Testament Studies from the University of Manchester, England.

Chapter VII

THE INSPIRATION OF THE
NEW TESTAMENT

The State of the Question

THE DOCTRINE OF INSPIRATION ought to be defined within the larger context of revelation itself. For more than a century, the prevailing climate of thought in philosophy and theology has been hostile to any construction of divine revelation which links it too intimately with truth and language. The rise of negative Biblical criticism which led directly to the rejection of Biblical infallibility cannot be traced to discoveries in the historical or textual sciences, but resulted from the intellectual mood dominating the nineteenth century which interpreted religion in simple evolutionary terms. Although the climate of current theology has changed radically, the older criticism, founded on a different base, remains. Negative criticism tends, now as it did before, to cast doubt upon the factual and conceptual side of divine revelation. By undermining the truth character of the record of revelation, criticism serves as handmaiden to a pseudo-theology which strives to understand revelation in non-conceptual terms. It serves, therefore, the older and the newer theological liberalism equally well.

The central issue in the question of New Testament authority stands far behind the question of inspiration. The real battle must be fought back at the fountainhead of theology, divine revelation itself. Is it possible to have "theology" at all, without truth communicated from God to finite man, and to know this truth without receiving it couched in language? A defense of Biblical inspiration today must come to grips with revelation as truth, and truth in language. A term commonly employed in this connection is "propositional revelation." It is not the happiest turn of phrase to describe the whole Biblical record, which includes literary forms in no sense strictly "propositional" (poetry, visions, events, theophanies), but the term enjoys one overwhelming virtue. It makes reference to a body of truth, however transmitted, which originates with God and which provides the subject matter of theology. Wordless revelation may be called "personal"; in reality it is mere mysticism. The very possibility of theology begins with the premise that the infinite personal God has drawn man up into a language covenant with Himself in which both personal and rational knowledge are exchanged. The modern assumption that revelation can be personal, without being to any degree informative, is unwarranted. Knowledge is a precondition to encounter and is provided in Scripture.

Almost without exception, modern theories of revelation are correlated to experience and not to truth. Some Protestant theologians draw the line of antithesis with Rome precisely at this point, namely propositional revelation. Evangelicals must side decisively with Rome in this issue. The dispute at the Reformation concerned the proper sources for and interpretation of divine revelation, with neither side questioning the *existence* of revealed truth, for this would negate the very feasibility of theology.[1] Yet despite the witness of historical theology, which so unanimously awards the Bible an objective authority, it is still a mark of "critical orthodoxy" to strike a dart in the breast of "fundamentalism." Seldom, however, does any spokesman for the new Protestant theology rise above the rattle of clichés to answer one simple question: does revelation convey truth about God, or is it just an ecstatic experience? Inspiration cannot profitably be discussed until an answer has been given. The stumblingblock of inspiration to some degree concerns matters of fact and concept in the text of Scripture, but it is also tightly tied to a prior decision about revelation. Until it is acknowledged that God has whispered information to His servants the prophets (Amos 3:7) about His plans (Genesis 18:17) and will (Deuteronomy 29:29), then the question of inspiration is beside the point. For the Gospel is a revealed message conveying information that saves, and therefore the question of inspiration assumes great importance.

The position which can offer hope to an ambivalent and ambiguous theology today is one which confesses the written Scriptures *as such* to possess revelational significance. No other view can satisfy the demands of the Biblical evidence, while rescuing theology from chaotic disintegration. As a prelude to the subject, it is appropriate to outline the dilemmas of three modern positions on the inspiration of the New Testament.

The salvation history school has been vocal in affirming its belief in God's saving acts in history. The uniqueness of the New Testament writing, it asserts, consists in their temporal relation adjacent to the period of revelation. No inspiration is postulated of the written products themselves. They represent only a human response to these events. The authority of the New Testament, however, cannot be founded on the mere fact that its writers lived within the period of revelation, for little can be said with finality from that fact alone about the precise nature and meaning of these acts. A word from God is needed to decipher and focus the historical data. Christians do treasure the New Testament as the vibrant testimony of those who were *there* when God bared His mighty arm to save. They also confess the Scripture to be far more than that — a permanent transcript of the inspired apostolic Word, which contains a record of truth, factual and conceptual, that can make man wise unto salvation.

The fatal weakness in *the Barthian approach* is the distance implied between the "word of God" and the Scripture.[2] The Bible may thus be both true and false at the same time, for the word of revelation is not regarded as a body of truth, but as an encounter with a Person. This oversimplified truism, however, does not solve the problem. A person cannot have knowledge of another, until the two have become acquainted, and this demands conceptual prior knowledge. If Scripture contains only human responses to divine encounters, theology has no grounds for any of its assertions, and a long dark shadow is cast over the length of its endeavor. The Bible as human word must have revelatory value, or theology is without source or norm. The confusion of modern theology regarding the truth of the Gospel is the tragic harvest reaped from the prior generation in losing the objective inspiration of the Scriptures.

The strange linguistic mysticism of Martin Heidegger in his recent mood has produced a hybrid in modern theology known as the *new hermeneutic*. Its starting point is the enigmatic belief that "all language reveals being." Applied to the New Testament, the written word is considered as the expression of a "subject," the container in which first century Christian experience is stored. The art of hermeneutics seeks to release the existential genie in the text, and recreate for the reader that original encounter. The whole approach boils down to a simple principle — one reads the New Testament text in order to enter upon a non-rational experience which might authenticate one's being! The concepts and facts in Scripture become important only as the literary remains of the primary "language event." The ideas may be mythological, the events legendary, it is argued, but the experience is real! This new movement represents a final stage in the deterioration of theology. From this point there will be no further opportunity of recovering the Gospel for modern men until the theologians themselves bow again before God, who speaks truth in His Word.

The moment is right for a careful restatement of the evangelical position on the inspiration of the New Testament, true to the deepest currents of Biblical teaching. The doctrine of its plenary inspiration rests upon the broadest foundations and sturdiest supports.

Scripture and the History of Salvation

When one contemplates the entire process of redemption, from the Abrahamic covenant to the Incarnation itself, it soon becomes apparent what a strategic role written Scripture played. The divine commentary on redemptive history was no incidental by-product, but was in fact an integral segment of it. This is the principle gained from observing the attitude of Christ and the apostles to the Old Testament. They regarded the written word of Scripture as the infallible utterance of the God who cannot lie

(John 10:35), a product of the Holy Spirit (II Peter 1:21), an effective transcript of revelation necessary to salvation (II Timothy 3:16). God's saving activity in the Old Testament epoch did not stop with special events or even utterances, but issued forth in a permanent verbal record of divine authority.

This simple fact has an extreme relevance for the inspiration of the New Testament, for it explains where Scripture is set in the pattern of revelation. Inspiration must be defended on too narrow a front, if appeal is made only to specific texts about it. First, one ought to be directed to the organism of revelation so easily observable in the New Testament itself. The Lord Jesus possessed primary authority (Matthew 7:29), but endowed certain of His followers with the power to bear witness to Himself in a unique way through the Spirit (Matthew 10:1; John 14:26; 16:13; Acts 1:21 f.; Hebrews 2:3, 4). The New Testament canon, though collected after the period of revelation, comprises documents written within it, and flowing from it. The instrument of divine revelation used by the Spirit to convert men's hearts today is the Scriptures. For, while special revelation was prior to and broader in content than Scripture, yet Scripture alone contains the true record of that revelation, sufficient to bring a man to saving faith. The pattern of divine revelation is clear. The triune personal God has disclosed His nature and will for man in a series of historical events and prophetic words, a selection of which the Spirit has secured in a written form.

Christianity was born a book-religion. It has a built-in doctrine of inspiration derived from the structure of Old Testament revelation. Inevitably Christianity created also a deposit of Scripture, a fixed verbal record of her revelation truth. In the minds of the earliest Christians, the fresh divine activity they were privileged to witness was the prolongation and culmination of a long redemptive process stretching into the distant past. The parallels between the period of Old Testament revelation and their own, between the prophets and the apostles, between the inspiration of Old Testament Scriptures and the partly oral, partly written, Gospel tradition, did not escape them. The subject of New Testament inspiration is properly opened at this point. "For if, as we have found, the authoritative witness of the New Testament bears out the unbreakable and inerrant character of the Old, how could that which forms an organic unit with the Old be of an entirely different character as regards the nature of its inspiration?"[3] As God crowned His initial work of redemption with infallible Scriptures, He has not failed so to do in honor of His more excellent work in Christ. This principle lies at the heart of the matter. God set a verbal canon, the Old Testament, even over His incarnate Son. Failure to accept the norm of Scripture over theology is tantamount to rejecting the speech and activity of God in history altogether.

THE PATTERN OF AUTHORITY IN THE NEW TESTAMENT

Needless to say, the authority of Scripture rests on the ultimate authority of God speaking, and of Jesus Christ, the incarnate Word. There is not a suggestion of any opposition existing between God and the Scriptures, or between the written and personal Word. Encounter and truth both play a part. The Bible is God's Word in human language. It does not compete with other modes and forms of revelation. Far from hindering the freedom of the divine authority, the Scriptures make the divine self-disclosure effective by conveying truth to the mind of man. Scripture presents, proclaims, uplifts, and exalts Jesus Christ.

An efficient way of penetrating to the core of the subject is to examine the history of revelation outlined in the New Testament. The important role of the apostle in shaping the life of the primitive churches is a matter of historical fact, yet here lies the clue for the quest. New Testament Scripture is not merely predictable, appropriate and necessary in abstraction. There actually appeared on the scene a group of men claiming to be instruments of revelation, namely, the apostles.[4] Their unique witness to Christ was an integral segment of divine revelation. As divinely appointed emissaries (Mark 3:14) and armed with special authority (Luke 9:1), the apostles went forth, equipped with the Spirit (Matthew 10:19; John 14-16); they went as witnesses of the resurrection (Acts 10:41), to declare to lost men an infallible message (13:47). Their witness to Christ was the foundation of Christianity from the very first (Ephesians 2:20; Matthew 16:18). There is no other way to explain the otherwise inexplicable note of authority in their correspondence. The publication of the Gospel was not left to chance. It was committed to a body of specially endowed individuals, whose word was law for the faith and life of primitive Christianity (I Timothy 6:20; II Timothy 1:14; 2:2). After their death (and to some extent even in their lifetime), this unique witness sounded from their writings. The New Testament canon marks off the boundary between Gospel and tradition. This transition from oral to written tradition is already indicated in the New Testament itself (II Thessalonians 2:15; II Peter 3:15).

A category of similar importance to the New Testament pattern is "tradition." This term refers to a deposit of saving truth (I Corinthians 15:3) originating ultimately with the Lord Himself (I Corinthians 11:23), and normative over human concepts (Colossians 2:8). In the narrow sense, "tradition" refers to the authoritative teaching about the person and work of Christ, the great events of His life and ministry (Luke 1:2), but includes the apostolic preaching as well. This "tradition" comprised the verbal word the Lord Jesus imposed on His Church. To this tradition, even the apostles were passive. It was "the faith once for all delivered to the saints" (Jude 3). The Gospel facts and the structure of its message were fixed. The tradition enjoyed authority from its ultimate origin, the Lord Jesus, and from those who conveyed it to the churches, the apostles. While claiming authority in his own right to legislate and teach, Paul also made joyous reference to the tradition he received. These two modes of authority were aspects of one, the authority of the risen Christ in history.

Three other themes in the New Testament have the closest relevance to inspiration: those of proclamation (*kerygma*), witness (*martyria*), and doctrine (*didaché*), and all three are closely interrelated. The proclamation of the Gospel includes both witness to historic events and appropriate doctrinal and ethical inferences. Preaching includes both an open statement of the truth (II Corinthians 4:2), and the demand for wholehearted response. Properly speaking, this *kerygma* is the Gospel in its fullest sense, embracing both fact and teaching (I Peter 1:25). In the earliest years it was largely oral, and gradually received a written form. The *kerygma* was the authority and norm of the first believers, and the New Testament today functions as the standard of apostolic Christianity.

The witness aspect of the gospel message is the guarantee of the factual and historical content. The basic criticism of the new existential theologies is that they violate the witness-character of the Gospel. Primarily *martyria* refers to the historical tangibility and perceptibility of the saving acts of God (I John 1:1-4), and this witness itself forms part of the authoritative proclamation. The apostolic witness to Christ was, by His own choosing, the final installment of the revelatory act of God (Acts 10:41). The apostolic words describing the Resurrection and Gospel are not merely human in origin; they are also words of the Spirit (I Corinthians 2:13; 14:37; I Thessalonians 2:13). Faith can rest securely upon the record of God's saving activity in history, because the Scripture itself is authenticated for integrity by inspired emissaries (John 19:35; 20:30; 21:24). As witnesses to Christ, the gospels are not accidental products of human ingenuity, but divinely given accounts of the historical reality out of which salvation issues.

The Gospel comes to expression also as doctrine (*didaché*). The word "doctrine" comprises both creedal and ethical teaching and includes a vast range of subjects, even as the Gospel embraces man and his world in all their aspects. Congregations were warned to adhere to the apostolic *didaché* and to continue in its truth (Romans 6:17; I Timothy 6:20). This *didaché* is no set of mere human opinions, but constitutes another form in which the *kerygma* takes shape. Divine revelation is not left suspended in mid-air, but finds expression in human language which safeguards and actualizes it. The New Testament is nothing other than the final verbalized resting place in which the infallible gospel message still confronts mankind.

THE SELF-WITNESS OF THE NEW TESTAMENT

Few students have attempted to deny the existence of a wide stream of teaching in the Bible about its own authority. Some have questioned the cogency of an appeal to it, preferring to rest their concept of inspiration on the observable data in it. Teaching on inspiration, however, *is* one of the data, and the whole question of authority is insoluble if that witness is ignored. What doctrine would stand if tested only by the critical scrutiny of an autonomous sinful man? Inspiration cannot fly in the face of the evidence; at the same time it should be defined, like other doctrines, in the light of the teachings of Christ and the apostles. If the current consensus of thought determined the validity of doctrines, the Christian faith would be identical with that consensus and theology would lose all right to a revelation claim. The doctrine of inspiration is not to be accommodated to the alleged difficulties of our age. This would forfeit the entire principle by which doctrine is established. The self-attestation of the Bible is indispensable in the task of framing the doctrine of inspiration, because it is asking in effect what the Lord and His apostles say about the matter. The Bible stands prior to any critical verdict man may make upon it. Indeed, these critical problems take on a different complexion when considered in the light of the inspiration taught in Scripture. The doctrine is established Biblically, and tested inductively.

The authority of the New Testament is grounded basically in the categories of revelation already discussed — proclamation, witness, doctrine. The four gospels provide a luminous witness to Jesus the Son of God. Their integrity rests ultimately upon the promise of the Lord to His apostles (John 16:12-15), and was protected by their preservation within a community which carefully guarded its historical remembrances. In the Epistles more especially the note of direct authority is clearly and insistently heard. The twin epistles of Paul to the church at Thessalonica, for example, give ample witness to this. Paul was grateful to God, that, when his preaching was received, it was not regarded as just another piece of human speculation, but was believed under the influence of the Holy Spirit (I Thessalonians 1:5) and accepted as the Word of God (2:13). Two important elements are present: the objective truth character of the message and the inner, authenticating work of the Spirit in the heart, enabling lost man to recognize the truth. This "word of God" refers to the total content of his teaching ministry among them (Acts 17:1-9). The teaching included both doctrine and morals (I Thessalonians 4:1 ff.). Because the Christians already knew the *divine* commandment on love, he wrote, there was no need for him to issue further authoritative teaching on that theme (4:9).

At the close of the letter, Paul *adjured* them (a strong term) to read his letter to all the brethren (5:27). Perhaps he wanted to put a stop to the practice of withholding the letter from certain individuals. At any rate, Paul insisted that his apostolic teaching was mandatory for all the congregation. The second letter confirms this impression. Paul again urged the people to stand firm and hold fast to "the traditions which you were taught by us, either by word of mouth or by letter" (II Thessalonians 2:15). A letter from him ranked in their minds on a par with the inspired utterance of a prophet (cf. 2:2). Failure to heed the contents of his instructions in the letter should be met with a stern reprimand (3:14). In order to stamp the letter with personal authority, Paul wrote the closing words in his own hand (3:17; cf. Colossians 4:18; Galatians 6:11). By so doing, Paul ensured its reception as the written injunctions of an apostle of Christ, an authority which continues to rule over the Church of God.

From the doctrine of inspiration, a certain range of legitimate inferences may safely be drawn.

The Scripture is inerrant and infallible. Modern reaction to these time-honored expressions varies from ridicule to sarcasm. Many feel that the terms unduly minimize the human element in the Bible. The terms are not themselves Biblical, yet they do, nonetheless, express a crucial aspect of the doctrine of inspiration; namely, that the Bible is wholly trustworthy and wholly true. No single term can suffice to render the thought adequately without further qualification. There is a degree of freedom consistent with infallibility. The terms do express, however, a proper faith in the divine origin of the Bible, and in the trustworthiness of God speaking. For this reason they can profitably be retained. In the last analysis, the offense is not directed toward the terminology alone, but against the reality they express, namely, an inspired verbal record of intelligible revelation.

Inspiration does not imply exhaustive knowledge of a subject, nor does infallibility mean superhuman perception. When someone says, "John is a Democrat," that statement is infallible, if John belongs to the Democratic party. It tells truth unerringly. But the assertion is not exhaustive. It does not inform us about the shade of his political beliefs, but for its general purpose, it is wholly true. Even the fullest revelation in Christ is only partial and yet it is wholly true (I Corinthians 13:12). Abram knew

God truly but not exhaustively. Inspiration does not level revelation off to a horizontal line. The line of revelation rises steadily and progressively in history. Infallibility does not negate this, but rather rescues believers from the wastelands of subjectivity in the realm of that genuine truth they possess from and about our Saviour God.

Inspiration does not suggest that the inspired penmen were necessarily conscious of the breathing of the Holy Spirit at the time of their writing and research. St. Luke and the Chronicler may have been unaware of their role as authors of Scripture, yet it is irrelevant to the question of their inspiration. One might as well object that Copernicus was conscious of shaping the history of science by his hypothesis. The doctrine of inspiration simply asserts that these writers *did* in fact contribute to the volume of inspired writings (whether or not they were aware of it) by the activity and providence of God. His activity is often known only through its effects. The effect in this case was the body of infallible Scripture. The mechanics of how they came to be composed and collected over the millennia of salvation history is a question of Biblical criticism, not of doctrine. In inspiration, whether the human will is more active or passive can only be surmised; the product is the same in any case — a document in language chosen by men and the Spirit, both human and divine.

Inspiration relates to the original text of Scripture. This inference is frequently challenged by an argument like this: No man has seen the originals. Did they correspond exactly in content to the extant copies? Such copies were pronounced infallible by Christ and the apostles. This opinion represents a misunderstanding. It is a fact which seems strange to some, that God did not protect the Scriptures from the corrupting influences of transmission. But evangelicals must speak of the "autographs" because inspiration concerns the *writers* not the *readers* (II Peter 1:21), and they feel the more confident in so doing, because the transmission of these documents has been nothing less than superb. Jesus' respect for the extant copies of Scripture is not proof of fallible originals, but a testimony to the providence of God so evident in textual criticism in preserving these documents over the centuries so free from error, that they can function as the originals did. Textual criticism requires no pessimism; for such corruption as there is can be easily detected and the text restored. This confidence is the basis of this science.

Inspiration sets certain limits upon the range of answers acceptable from negative Biblical criticism. It is not a question of muffling the discipline, but of deciding whether to accept believing or unbelieving criticism. Critical speculation is valid only within the recognition of inspiration. This doctrine is a relevant fact underneath every critical endeavor, to condition the methods employed and examine the results. No hypothesis which attributes gross historical error and anachronism to the gospel writers, no theory which derides the apostles for inconsistency or fallacy, no pseudepigraphic view of authorship which directly contradicts the inner claim of a New Testament book — none of these critical conclusions can be accepted because they contradict the testimony of God Himself in the Scripture. The critic may appeal to some Biblical phenomenon in support of his thesis, but, notwithstanding, an uncertain human opinion is here preferred to the integrity of God. It is more likely that man has erred than that God has lied.

THE HUMANITY OF THE NEW TESTAMENT

For those familiar with the problems of inspiration, a critical phase of the question is reached at this point. Some evangelicals have shown a certain impatience with those who claim to uncover marks of human frailty on the sacred page. Failure to admit traits of human authorship has discredited the Biblical doctrine in the eyes of many, causing them to flee orthodoxy with undue haste. However precise dogmatics may be in deducing the doctrine of inspiration from the witness of the Bible, it cannot for long remain indifferent to the gains of a close honest study of the text. Of course, there is the real danger of granting the critic that infallibility denied to the Bible. After all, the evidence is not all in by any means, and critical opinion is never final. Yet it is a fair question to ask what "infallibility" means in relation to the actual phenomena of the Bible. Infallibility alone is rather abstract, and does not automatically afford solutions to critical inquiries. The ensuing discussion will explore a very limited selection of problems in order both to offer concrete solutions and also illustrate methodology for sound Biblical criticism.

Tensions do exist between the divine and human sides of the Bible. It would be unfair to suggest that this "dark side" of Bible study is broader than it is. It is proper neither to exaggerate nor to minimize its existence, but simply to recognize it. A few human traits may briefly be listed: the deliberate omission or inclusion of details in a historical narrative to create a certain impact on the reader; a pre-scientific description of the world; an arrested time factor in eschatological teaching; a variety of text types employed in the citation of the Old Testament; arguments styled in a Rabbinic mode of thought; an occasional difference of incidental detail in a gospel story; a lack of meticulous precision in detail. These traits of human authorship have all been freely admitted by those holding to the high doctrine of inspiration. In some cases they relate to the historical context in which the revelation was given, in others to the purpose of that revelation. In no case do they prevent or hinder the functioning of God's Word under the testimony of the Spirit. The precise relation of the human and divine elements will never be wholly comprehended. But inspiration signifies that God has efficaciously willed the Scripture in the form in which we have received it. Infallibility is complex, not simple. God is not overcome by the human material He sanctifies, yet neither does He choose to eliminate from the record the clear marks of human authorship.

Before dealing with three major topics in this connection, two smaller matters held to be contradictory to infallibility should be considered. These illustrate the method of dealing with minor criticisms, which rely upon some false or one-sided interpretation of a passage. For example, Jude 14 is often held up to demonstrate how Jude's canon included an uninspired book, First Enoch, and how this Biblical epistle thereby shows its human fallibility. Is it certain, however, that Jude is quoting from I Enoch as an inspired book; or further, that he teaches that Enoch actually uttered these very words? Surely not! Jude simply employs the sentiment contained in the saying to refute a heresy, and does not thereby define the limits of the canon. As an individual, Jude considered the apocryphal books of some value. There is no reason to infer from this that he "erred" in his writing.

On a different key, some critics take exception to the alleged grammatical barbarities in the Apocalypse of John. The anxiety, however, is unnecessary. The author of Revelation violates accepted grammatical canons, not out of his abysmal ignorance of Greek, but in his attempt to imitate the style of the Old Testament by archaizing his own. He surely succeeded in his aim, and cannot be charged with error on that account.

Such minor attacks upon the integrity of Scripture will not make any deep impression on the mind of him who is aware of the Biblical doctrine of inspiration, and gripped by its sublime depth and power. There remain three larger issues which concern the essential literary and cultural form of the New Testament.

Historical Narration

If drawing is the "art of omission," so also is the writing of history. The Bible does not set down accounts for history's sake. Its narratives are marked by deliberate omissions and emphases which weight the account in the direction of some theological lesson. This is common sense history. It does not enjoy an infinite perception or perspective. From a purely chronological point of view, this history may be inadequate. From the viewpoint of the divine intent in revelation, the account is sufficient and effective. The shape of the historical situation is defined for the instruction of God's people, and represents the original event fairly from one angle at least. The history, though incomplete, is nevertheless reliable and true. Even an omission which might have disturbed the contemporaries of the event is justified in the light of the larger context as God wants it seen. Matthew, for example, assembled his material in a catechetical plane, rather than a strictly chronological one. Luke omitted large sections of Mark as unnecessary for his portrait of Christ. John openly admitted his extreme selectivity. The order of events in Jesus' life and even the precise wording of His sayings are subject to some fluidity. Acts focused so closely upon the key apostles, Peter and Paul, as to suggest that these two carried the brunt of the mission. In no way do these observations jeopardize the integrity and infallibility of the New Testament.

Certain questions about the accuracy of the New Testament record are still being asked, but negative form-criticism survives chiefly because it is the handmaiden of existential theology and serves to bolster its assault on the historical and rational elements in Christianity. The negative regard for New Testament history has little to do with the historical realities therein. It is more of a frame of mind, difficult to change. A brief glance at the impact of Christ, the centrality of the apostles, and the brief time-lag between event and record, should be sufficient to convince an honest student of the integrity of the gospels. Fortunately the climate is slowly changing. There have been clear reversals of criticism respecting the Fourth Gospel, and further research into the Jewish backgrounds of all the gospels is shifting New Testament studies toward more conservative conclusions.

As for the book of Acts, the archaeological work of William Ramsay sparked an attitude of highest regard for the historical integrity of the account. Although commentaries do appear which choose to ignore the influence of Ramsay (e.g. Conzelman and Haenchen), the opinion that Luke is consistently and minutely accurate is widely held. There is, however, at least one detail in Acts where a historical blunder is still suspected (Acts 5:36). The point concerns the sequence of the rebellions of Judas and Theudas found in the speech attributed to Gamaliel. The Jewish historian, Josephus, refers to both men, but dates Theudas long after Judas, during the office of Fadus, about A.D. 45, a decade after the speech was given in Jerusalem. Either Luke committed two errors — a serious anachronism and mistake in order — or he committed none. In view of Luke's regular accuracy, is it not conceivable that Luke is referring to a Theudas, otherwise unknown to us, who did live before Judas in A.D. 6? The question illustrates a hermeneutical principle: when all the evidence is not yet available, and critical opinion varies considerably, it is unwise to jettison inerrancy prematurely. Evangelicals need have no alarm at the current trends in historical research.

PSEUDEPIGRAPHY

Conservative evangelicals have never been content with solutions for the problem of authorship which involve pseudepigraphy, which would involve a pious fraud, a literary hoax. Alternate solutions have been sought in the direction of a secretary hypothesis, or re-editing by a beloved disciple. There is certainly a difference between the literary form of Ecclesiastes, which sets forth Solomon as the embodiment of wisdom, and the gross deception implied in II Peter, where critics allege that an intimate letter replete with personal allusions claiming the authority of the Apostle Peter was foisted on the Church by someone who had no connection with Peter at all. In such hypotheses it is often tacitly assumed that pseudepigraphy was a normal and accepted literary device of the time. This is, however, fallacious. An elder in Asia was repudiated because he tried to honor Paul by writing a harmless tract in his name. Historically it is most unlikely that the Church would have tolerated any letter purporting to come from the mind, if not pen, of an apostle, which could not justify this claim.

In the case of II Peter, the view has been expressed (by Chaine), that the writer was Peter's disciple who composed the letter in his name out of genuinely apostolic teaching he knew. In view of the linguistic problems, this theory has some merit. Other moderate scholars propound a similar view for the Pastorals; namely, that a follower of Paul composed the letters out of material which the apostle himself had prepared for writing just before his death. Obviously these theories do not present the same difficulties to infallibility that pseudepigraphy does. We should, however, be cautious even here. Is there an urgent need to postulate this distance between the apostolic word and the Biblical text in these cases? We must not surrender direct apostolic authorship too readily. The good intentions of a loyal disciple are no substitute for the words of a great apostle, if so they be.

In point of fact, the case against the authenticity of the Pastorals has been slipping badly in recent years. Of the four great objections raised against them a century ago — the historical, ecclesiastical, doctrinal, linguistic — only the last one is much discussed today, and even that is most inconclusive under the shadow of a possible secretary hypothesis. Second Peter is the most difficult book to defend against the charge of pseudepigraphy. While it is more like I Peter than any other New Testament book, it differs from it greatly, and its relation to Jude (or its

source) is problematic. But such difficulties even here are far
from insuperable, and the "synoptic problem" between II Peter
and Jude is free from negative overtones.

How does the doctrine of inspiration touch upon this question?
It does so at the point of trustworthiness. The theory of literary
forgery imputes to the New Testament a built-in lie. The motives
of the author are not relevant, for a noble motive does not make
a deception non-fraudulent. Canonicity and authenticity are
closely bound together. The reason II Peter and the Pastorals
are in our New Testament canon is the conviction held by the
early Church that these were genuine. If this were demonstrated not to be the case, the grounds for recognizing their
inspiration would be lacking. If one continues to regard these
books as canonical and inspired, he must also seek to vindicate
their integrity. It is for this reason inconceivable that pseudepigraphy is a literary form employed by the Spirit in the Scriptures.

CULTURALLY-CONDITIONED TRUTH

Inspiration secures the text of Scripture and hermeneutics
grapples with it. "Hermeneutics" is the science of interpretation,
the extraction of truth from the text. Upon examining the New
Testament it becomes at once apparent that much of its teaching
is framed in a temporary cultural setting that no longer exists.
Mild discomfort is then felt over the plenary view of inspiration,
and the general applicability of Scripture. The problem might
be called "transculturalization" to coin a term — how to render
the full impact of the inspired text for the new generation with
fresh needs. All truth is in some sense culturally conditioned.
There is no possibility of extracting the existential "core" of
Scripture and reclothing it with modern myths. This process
succeeds only in removing the heart from the Gospel. Two steps
are required of the exegete: mastery of the meaning of the text in
its historical context, and appreciation of the requirements of the
culture in which he stands. Both skills are necessary for good
interpretation.

The Spirit produced the Bible over a long period of time within
an ancient cultural complex. Failure to appreciate this had led
liberals to apostasy and some conservatives to absurdity. Be-

cause the Bible speaks in the language of pre-Copernican science, it is not just to charge it with error. Inspiration did not bestow upon the writer a modern mind, nor correct his idiosyncrasies. Nor did it smuggle into the text clever premonitions of modern discovery to satisfy the delight of curiosity seekers. The Bible speaks in the straightforward language of its day the wonderful words of life. In the time of Paul, it was customary for married women to wear veils as the sign of subjection to their husbands. He insisted on the continuance of the practice in order to defend the family at Corinth from further decay (I Corinthians 11:10). It is not incumbent on us to employ these same symbols, if we recognize the principle in another way. In exegesis and application it is unwise to neglect the social climate of the time. The universal teachings of Biblical ethics ought to have strict priority over the local expressions of them. Footwashing, for example, was a custom in ancient Palestine, which Jesus adopted to demonstrate humility and love. The local expression has no significance in a country where sandals are not worn, but the principle of love has universal significance.

The Bible addresses man as a historically conditioned person with a message of truth pertaining to his life. It therefore takes up the languages, images, and thought-forms of living men. These human elements are elevated to higher divine service in the sacramental activity of revelation. One facet in our universe of discourse is taken to represent one facet in God's universe, and so truth is conveyed by analogy. The task of translation is always necessary. It is only the common procedure employed in understanding any ancient book and thinker.

There are shadows on the record of Scripture, which ought to be squarely faced, but they do not cast doubt upon the veracity of the written Word. Rather, they stimulate inquiry after clarification and the search for the mind of the Spirit in the matter. There is no need to close one's eyes to the actual phenomena of Scripture, any more than there is need to reject the infallibility of the Bible because of the pressures of negative criticism.

In its rejection of infallibility, modern theology has found itself uncertain as to the objective reality of revelation at all. Theology which operates only within the circle of human concepts and experiences has no transcendent reference point. If this were true, the vast majority of Christian thinkers in history have been deluded, and the faith of millions has been vain. Only a return to the Biblical doctrine of inspiration will heal the deadly sickness in the theology of today. Granting that the Bible is true, God's purpose to visit and redeem His people in act and word was effective, and it can be proclaimed with joy and confidence.

THE MESSAGE OF THE WORD
John H. Gerstner

John H. Gerstner

John H. Gerstner is Professor of Church History at Pittsburgh Theological Seminary. He is the author of *Ephesians, Steps to Salvation*: *The Evangelistic Message of Jonathan Edwards, The Theology of the Major Sects*, and *Reasons for Faith*. He holds the degrees of Ph.D. from Harvard University and D.D. from Tarkio College.

Chapter VIII

THE MESSAGE OF THE WORD

FOR SOME TIME men have questioned the reliability of the Bible's presentation of the historical and scientific setting of its message. Today, these men question the religious message itself. For them the Bible is no longer the "infallible rule" even of "faith and practice." It is regarded as fallible no less in matters of faith than in matters of fact. Markus Barth's *Conversation With the Bible* illustrates this widespread, far-reaching change of outlook by otherwise reverent Bible scholars.

When one speaks of the message of the Bible, some immediately say, "Which message?" They believe that there are many messages in the Bible; almost as many messages as messengers. There is the message of Paul, the message of Peter, and the message of James. Jesus' message is thought to be different from Moses', and Ezekiel's is not the same as Amos'. In fact, one part of Ezekiel is not the same as another part of Ezekiel, and when one mentions Paul, which Paul is it of whom he is speaking? they ask. Many moderns believe with Rudolf Bultmann that the message of Jesus is hardly separable or even distinguishable from the message of the church which was put into His mouth by later interpolators. The Bible, it is taught, is not the Word of God, but many words of man about God.

THE CASE FOR MANY MESSAGES

Salvation itself is presented as bestowed by God but elsewhere as achieved by man through works of the law. There seems to

165

be considerable agreement among many modern theologians that the Bible essentially is an account of the history of salvation, or *Heilsgeschichte*. It would seem, therefore, that on at least one point the message of the Bible is unified. It should tell a single story and that story would concern salvation. If, however, one looks more closely at this apparent unity of the Bible as *Heilsgeschichte*, he discovers that it is a unity in name only. If the Bible is the history of salvation, then salvation must have some specific meaning for this term to indicate a unity of theme. The *Heilsgeschichte* scholars when asked for the meaning of salvation offer conflicting answers, or no valid answer. They affirm that salvation itself is presented in the Pauline theology as bestowed by God, but that elsewhere it is achieved by man through the work of the law.

For example, they say that, according to Ezekiel, salvation is by man. These scholars quote his teaching: "When the righteous man turneth away from his righteousness, and committeth iniquity, and dieth therein; in his iniquity that he hath done shall he die. Again, when the wicked man turneth away from his wickedness that he hath committed, and doeth that which is lawful and right, he shall save his soul alive" (Ezekiel 18:26, 27). According to this ancient prophet (as some modern scholars understand him), man saves himself by being righteous and thereby making himself acceptable to Yahweh. This is self-salvation, or salvation by works. On the other hand, however, the Apostle Paul, at least in Romans and Galatians, states salvation by pure grace in as clear form as it can be expressed according to these same scholars. Does Paul not say, for example, in Romans 4:5: "But to him that worketh not, but believeth on him that justifieth the ungodly, his faith is reckoned for righteousness"?

According to Galatians, "As many as are of the works of the law are under a curse: for it is written, Cursed is every one who continueth not in all things that are written in the book of the law, to do them. Now that no man is justified by the law before God, is evident: for, The righteous shall live by faith" (Galatians 3:10, 11). So Paul is far from believing that man can make himself righteous or save himself by his work. He goes so far as to deny that man does anything which is in any way acceptable to God. All are totally dependent upon the sheer and sovereign mercy of God. Thus, some advocates of *Heilsgeschichte* understand the presentation of salvation according to Ezekiel as salvation by works, and according to Paul as salvation by grace.

The same contrast is found between Paul and James in the New Testament. This shows that there is not only a supposed conflict between the Old Testament and the New, but that *Heilsgeschichte* projects an inconsistency into the structure of the New Testament itself. For example, some think that they find evidence that Jesus' teaching is like the alleged teaching of Ezekiel on salvation, while other strands of His message are like Paul's salvation by pure grace. Jesus, telling the parable of the Pharisee (Luke 18:10 ff.), indicates that the publican could not claim any good works but was a despicable individual despised by the Pharisee. When he beat upon his breast and asked God to have mercy upon him, a sinner, he went down to his house justified; on the other hand, the Pharisee, who was morally admirable in the Jewish community, was not even heard by the Lord because of his self-righteous prayer. By this teaching Jesus seems to advocate pure gracious salvation, not only without works, but in spite of very evil works. On the other hand, Jesus said to the rich young ruler (18:18 ff.), when the latter inquired about inheriting eternal life, "You know the commandments," and then He listed a few of them. Presumably this shows that Jesus was teaching legalism; namely, that by virtue of obeying the commandments a person inherits eternal life. Of course, such legalism would be in sharpest contradiction not only to what these scholars agree that Paul taught, but also to what they admit Jesus Himself taught on other occasions.

Not only is there considerable disunity in understanding the meaning of salvation, but even "history" (*Geschichte*) in the expression "history of salvation" or *Heilsgeschichte* is diversely understood by some scholars. Some have maintained that salvation could not occur in history at all. If God's gracious revelation did occur in history, they think that it would be contaminated by finite limitations and by the sinfulness of the men who act out our history. Others, who will not allow a complete divorce between history and salvation, but insist that this salvation must take place in our space and time, nevertheless do attempt to some degree to keep history separate from the salvation. The debates about the early Karl Barth and his "rim of history" are not yet ended. *Historicismus*, or thé purely subjective creation of history, is the hallmark of twentieth century philosophy of history which separates it from the nineteenth century so drastically.

Absolute determination and absolute freedom are often thought to be contradictions in the message of the Bible. Some parts of Holy Scripture, it is said, teach that God determines with utter precision and complete fixity everything which is to come to pass (Psalm 33:11; Proverbs 16:33; Isaiah 46:10, 11; Matthew 10:30; Ephesians 1:11). This determination extends to the actions of men and angels alike and, therefore, indicates that their decisions are predetermined by God. On the other hand, many see in various parts of Scripture an equally clear statement of the spontaneous freedom of men and angels. Appeal is made especially to the "whosoever will" passages (John 3:16, 36; 7:17) which seem to say that all men make decisions spontaneously, and that such decisions were not made from all eternity. So, it seems to some, the message of the Bible is that God or man is the arbiter of human destiny, depending on what text one reads.

Atonement and justice are conflicting themes in the Bible. Some men see both *Karma* and atonement taught in the same context. *Karma* denotes the law of works and retribution: all men are to be judged according to their works, and evil works must necessarily be punished, good works rewarded. In the language of the Bible, "The wages of sin is death" (Romans 6:23); and again, "God is not mocked: for whatsoever a man soweth, that shall he also reap" (Galatians 6:7). Such passages as these are construed by many to teach that a man is to be saved or damned strictly and exclusively on the basis of what he does.

There is no room for mercy or suspension of judgment or showing of favor when evil demands necessary and inevitable punishment. Nevertheless, the Bible does set forth a Gospel of good news that God forgives sinners. He does so, according to the Bible, by delivering up Christ for our offenses and raising Him again for our justification (Romans 4:25). This means that salvation rests not on works but on faith, not on what a person does but on whom he believes.

Here again a contradiction seems to be built into the heart of the message of Christianity. Man saves or damns himself by what he does, and there is no possibility of works having anything other than their legitimate consequences for good or evil; while, on the other hand, the very center of the message is the declaration that in spite of sins a person may receive eternal life.

Man's ability to act with respect to Christ is diversely represented by the Bible according to certain interpreters. Thus there are some Biblical statements which say that except a man be born again he cannot see or he cannot enter the kingdom of God (John 3:3, 5), and that he who commits sin is the bond servant of sin (John 8:34). The leopard that cannot change his spots and the Ethiopian who cannot change his skin constitute the prophet's analogy (Jeremiah 13:23) of the sinner's inability to change his character. According to the Bible, man is likened to a bad tree which must bring forth bad fruit (Matthew 7:18 ff.). Consequently, men as sinners are indisposed and unable to believe in Jesus Christ. In their present state they will certainly disbelieve and reject Him. While this seems clear in some passages, other passages seem, to such interpreters, to teach the opposite: "Him that cometh to me I will in no wise cast out" (John 6:37); "Believe on the Lord Jesus Christ and thou shalt be saved" (Acts 16:31). All such statements teach implicitly, it is said, that man is able to believe and be saved.

These contrasts could be continued indefinitely, but as a final example one should note that there are divergent opinions about the Bible in the Bible. There are many statements in the Bible which teach its inspiration by the Spirit of God. Holy men of old being moved by the Holy Spirit wrote the Scripture (II Peter 1:21). Many times the words of men, prophets, and apostles are set forth by the phrase, "Thus saith the Lord." On approximately 3,000 occasions the Bible refers to itself as the Word of God. Nevertheless, it is the man Isaiah who said, "Thus saith the Lord," and it is Paul, the Jew of Tarsus, who wrote Romans, which means that men are the authors of the Word of God. It is constantly evident that the books of Scripture were not handed down from heaven written by the finger of God, but were the compositions of human authors. Therefore, argue some, the Bible is not the Word of God about man, but the word of man about

God. Consequently these two diametrically opposed views of the Bible are drawn presumably from the Bible itself. There are even two messages of the Bible about the Bible; namely, "The Bible is the Word of God," versus "The Bible is the word of man."

THE CASE FOR ONE MESSAGE

Does the Bible have one message, or does it have many messages? Does it speak with one voice or with many voices? Does it say one thing or many things? Is it one story or many stories? Can one legitimately ask the question, "What does the Bible teach?" or must he rephrase the question to say, "What does this part of the Bible teach?" Is there a unity of testimony or a Babel of confusion? Is it one Bible or is it sixty-six books under that heading?

In spite of all that has been said and of all apparent evidence to the contrary, one can maintain with confidence that the Bible has one message, speaks with one voice, tells one story, unfolds one plan of salvation, has one view of itself; is, in fact, one book, one Bible, one Word of God. This may be easier said than demonstrated, but the concept that the Bible has many different messages is erroneous.

The message of the Bible is unitary regarding salvation. The Bible does not teach that salvation is by man and also that salvation is by God. The Bible teaches, as all agree, that salvation originates with God. What then about Biblical statements which seem to teach conflictingly that salvation is by man, or by the works of the law? A close examination of the Bible reveals that it nowhere declares that men may be saved by good works. It says, to be sure, "This do and thou shalt live" (cf. Leviticus 18: 5). But it indicates also that men are not disposed to doing those things whereby they may live. Paul stresses in Galatians (3:10) and James also (2:10) that to sin in one detail is to violate the entire law. Since man sins in all respects he is never able to keep the law. In other words, the Bible is simply setting forth the standard by which a man would be acceptable to God if he could meet it. It says also that in his present sinful state, man is not able to do these things at all. His only hope of salvation is, therefore, not what he can do, but what God can do for him. In other words, the very law itself was given as a tutor to bring men to Christ for salvation, rather than to lead them from Christ to a substitute way of salvation.

The error of the scholars who fancy that they see a legalism in this strain of the Bible is in their jumping to the conclusion that because the Bible says, "This do and thou shalt live," it therefore implies that man is morally able in his present state so to do. It does not so imply, and it states frankly that man is in bondage to evil. Consequently, it does not envisage or teach that men can actually save themselves by their works. This reminder of the acceptability of man to God by perfect works carries with it a reminder at the same time that man is not now perfect. He is, therefore, shut up to another way of salvation; namely, the way of grace. That which looks to superficial observers as a contradiction is seen to be harmonious. It is not only not a contradiction but is in the closest possible interrelation and unity. The way of salvation is by grace alone, and nothing shows this so clearly as convincing man how unable he is to save himself by his own efforts.

The Bible has one message on history. It does not teach two kinds of history any more than it sets forth two plans of salvation. While it affirms that salvation is of the Lord, it shows also that salvation is wrought in the context of human life. Jesus Christ becomes a true man. He lives a genuine human life in a well-known part of the world, dies on a cross, is buried in a tomb, rises and ascends. These are all genuinely historical happenings that constitute the very center of the redemptive activity. The notion that this history has to be a special kind of history, a type of history different from our calendar history, is nowhere intimated in Holy Scripture. Such a concept is obviously a deduction from certain philosophical presuppositions which is subsequently read into the Biblical narrative and distorts its interpretation. Likewise, to say that God cannot act relative to human history without being relativized or humanized is a gratuitous assumption. That God is necessarily contaminated by sin when He acts on the heart of man is no sounder than saying that the rays of the sun are made impure by shining on offal.

In no case in which the Bible is presented as giving two or more different messages is this more palpably gratuitous than in the sovereignty-freedom matter. It is assumed rather than proven that the two teachings of the Bible (God is sovereign; man is free) are incompatible and therefore constitute two different and conflicting messages. The Bible simply says that God sovereignly brings all things to pass and that man spontaneously and without compulsion makes his decisions. It is immediately assumed by some that these two propositions cannot both be true, and therefore that the Bible is presenting two faces to the world.

Before attributing two messages to the Bible on the sovereignty-freedom theme it behooves one to demonstrate that these are two in actuality and not merely in the critic's mind. If one tries to show that these are mutually exclusive ideas he will give up in despair.

Divine sovereignty and human freedom are not inherently contradictory. The Bible is not saying either "God is sovereign — God is not sovereign"; nor is it saying, "Man is free — man is not free." Such messages would indeed be two; in fact, they would not be two but none, for each would cancel the other and leave no message remaining. Saying that God is sovereign does not necessarily mean that man is not free; nor does saying that man is free necessarily imply that God is not sovereign. The teaching of the Bible assuredly involves a mystery if God's sovereignty co-exists with man's freedom and if man's choices do not cancel God's decisions. A mystery, however, is not a contradiction, but something only partly known or understood; a contradiction is something totally unknown and unknowable. Once again men have contrived their own problems which they cannot solve until they realize that these *are* contrived and not real.

There is only one message on atonement. The error which sees two Biblical messages on the atonement is even more egregious than that which sees two messages in the divine sovereignty-human freedom teaching. The error in the latter originates from a gratuitous assumption of a conflict without any justification of the assumption. One could not say that divine sovereignty strictly requires human freedom, but merely that it does not necessarily exclude it. To the alleged contradiction between atonement and justice one may reply that these are not only not mutually exclusive concepts, but that atonement actually requires justice for its very meaning. Both are necessary, not merely allowable.

The Bible teaching about atonement presupposes rather than opposes the necessity of justice. First, it is the inexorable necessity of justice that requires an atonement by sacrifice if there is to be any forgiveness. God will "by no means clear the guilty," the Bible says (Exodus 34:7) because he is "of purer eyes than to behold evil" (Habakkuk 1:13). Since this absolutely just God did love the world, He gave his only Son . . . (John 3:16), and He delivered him up for us all (Romans 4:25). Jesus "was wounded for our transgressions, he was bruised for our iniquities; the chastisement of our peace was upon him; and with his stripes we are healed" (Isaiah 53:5); he was forsaken of the Father (Psalm 22:1; Matthew 27:46; Mark 15:34). Mere forgiveness of sins would have sufficed to reconcile men if the justice of God were dispensable; because it is not, atonement is necessary. On the basis of the atonement reconciliation is offered to men. It was because "God was in Christ reconciling the world" that the apostle could cry: "Be ye reconciled to God." It is because He who knew no sin became sin that we may become the "righteousness of God in him." "Who shall lay anything to the charge of God's elect?" is the question to which the Bible gives the answer: "It is God that justifieth. Who is he that condemneth? It is Christ that died, yea rather, that was raised from the dead, who is even at the right hand of God, who also maketh intercession for us" (Romans 8:33, 34).

In many ways the notion that the Bible gives two messages on the bondage-freedom question is the most surprising of all. While it is difficult to state the reconciliation of these two lines of teaching, it is relatively easy to understand. Every man is personally and experientially acquainted with this freedom-bondage motif in his own soul. Not only does the alcoholic know that he *cannot resist* the cup but he also knows that *he* cannot resist the cup. He knows the application to himself of the words: "for not what I would, that do I practise; but what I hate, that I do" (Romans 7:15). There is, in his experience, a simultaneous loathing and loving of the forbidden. Usually it is a loathing of the consequences of the thing and a loving of the thing itself. The alcoholic and all other sinners experience what Professor Boring of Harvard and others speak of as "cognitive dissonance." This refers to a disparity between what a man knows that he should do ("cognitive" element) and what he actually does ("dissonance" element).

"Cognitive dissonance" is the experience of the normal (sinful but not schizophrenic) man. One should be able to understand in thought what he daily experiences in life. Why should it be a contradiction constituting two divergent messages for the Bible to teach that man is hopelessly in bondage while responsibly free? In the last analysis, a man would not be in bondage if he were not free, for if he were not free he would not be a man. But suppose a person does actually love and incline to the evil, as the Bible says. His free, voluntary choice would inevitably be in accordance with that which he loves. He could not, as Jonathan Edwards has so clearly shown in his *Freedom of Will*, incline to that to which he is not inclined, prefer that which he does not prefer, choose that which he does not choose. All this is freedom, for freedom is to choose according to one's nature, but then where is the bondage? If a person knows that what he loves is evil and what he hates is good (as the Bible says), will this not make him chafe? Will not his mind, his conscience, his very body be outraged by the choices he freely makes? Karl Barth may say that sin is an "ontological impossibility," but the sinner thinks and experiences it every day. The free man in bondage is one man, and the Bible which describes him does so in one and not two messages: man is in bondage to himself.

Last of all, the Bible bears a united witness to itself. When it claims to be both the Word of God and the inspired word of men it is not stating two divergent messages but two harmonious aspects of the one message; namely, that the Bible is the Word of God written by inspired men. All concede that the Bible claims to be the Word of God. Many do not believe that the Bible is the Word of God, but none can doubt that the Bible so represents itself, as was shown above by various texts. With respect to man's part in the writing of the Bible there is also agreement among all up to a point. It is generally believed that there were men such as Samuel, David, Isaiah, James and John who wrote the various books of the Bible. While this fact is accepted, two different conclusions are drawn from it. Some say that the human authorship of the Bible, which the Bible itself affirms, shows that God Himself cannot be the author of it; yet the Bible also claims that God is its author. Hence it is alleged that there are two messages of the Bible about the Bible.

Another conclusion, however, may be drawn from the undisputed fact that the Bible was written by men. These men wrote what God wanted them to write so that their words were also His words. The Bible itself not only teaches, as already shown, that these men did speak and write God's Word, but it states how they did so. The Bible explains this process by the doctrine of inspiration, God's breathing into the Bible writers who consequently spoke not merely from themselves, but as "holy men of God . . . moved by the Holy Ghost" (I Peter 1:21). No one can say such an inspiration is not a possibility, and what must be conceded as a possibility the Bible says is the actuality.

The main point of the present argument is not whether the Bible is the Word of God and/or the word of man, but simply to show that it says it is both and does not contradict itself in so saying. The reader may have observed that the thought-situation on this point is somewhat different than on the others. With respect to these other matters various scholars actually do think that the Bible is giving two different messages. With respect to the Bible's testimony about itself men tend to recognize that there is really no question of two divergent messages, but they contend that there ought to be! Speaking candidly, most scholars will readily grant that the Bible teaches both that it is the Word of God and that it is the word of (or through) men. They actually regard these statements as mutually contradictory and argue that both cannot be true. They, not the Bible, think that the Bible must say that is is exclusively the Word of God or else say that it is wholly the word of man. It is enough to observe here that virtually all recognize that the Bible teaches two complementary facets of truth about itself, and not two divergent ones. It is the critics and not the Bible who say but do not prove that there are two messages here.

In spite of contentions to the contrary from all sides, there is only one Bible and one message in that one Bible. There is one God and none beside Him. This one God has revealed Himself in His one and only Son, the Lord Jesus Christ, the one Saviour of one mankind. This has been done in one history of the one redemption formulated in the one covenant of grace. It is offered and applied to the one mankind bound together in one sin and one sinfulness. There is one Gospel for one world. There is one way of justification for one and the same kind of sinner by one and the same kind of God. God is one, the Bible is one and the message is one.

The student of the one *Living Word of Revelation* may begin almost where he pleases. Starting with God, in that divine light he may see light; or he may begin with man and follow a pointing finger, "Behold the Lamb of God that taketh away the sin of the world" (John 1:29). He may view the one Bible from the angle of the one covenant of grace or see it from the vista of the unitary history of redemption. Contemplating the divine sovereignty he may behold it working itself out in the intricacies of a providence by which we live and move and have our being, and which becomes the framework of the spontaneity of human freedom. He may begin his pilgrimage from Paradise Lost and go on to Paradise Regained, and ultimately lose himself in the splendors of the saints gathered around the crystal sea, singing the praises of the Lamb that was slain from the foundation of the world.

The Bible in which God has clothed His revelation of Himself is like the seamless garment in which the Son of man was clothed. To tear apart the Bible is to rend the robe in which the deity is dressed. What God has joined together let not man rend asunder. When men gather together to raise a tower to heaven the result is a Babel of confusion of tongues and of messages. When God speaks, His Word is yea and amen — one Word, one Message, one God. And His Church is one in Him, "endeavouring to keep the unity of the Spirit in the bond of peace. There is one body, and one Spirit, even as ye were called in one hope of your calling; one Lord, one faith, one baptism, one God and Father of all, who is over all, and through all, and in all" (Ephesians 4:3-6).

THE PRAGMATIC
CONFIRMATION OF
SCRIPTURAL AUTHORITY

John F. Walvoord

John F. Walvoord

John F. Walvoord is President of Dallas Theological Seminary, having served the Seminary in various capacities since 1936. He is the author of *The Holy Spirit, The Return of the Lord, The Thessalonian Epistles, The Millennial Kingdom, Revelation,* and many other books, and was a member of the committee appointed by Oxford University Press to revise the Scofield Reference Bible. He holds the degrees of Th.D. from Dallas Theological Seminary and D.D. from Wheaton College, Illinois.

Chapter IX

THE PRAGMATIC CONFIRMATION OF SCRIPTURAL AUTHORITY

BELIEF IN THE VERBAL AND PLENARY INSPIRATION of the Holy Scriptures has unquestionably had a pragmatic influence on Christian faith and experience. Pragmatic philosophy as advanced by C. S. Peirce, William James, and John Dewey, teaching that truth is to be tested pre-eminently by the practical consequences of belief in it, is quite insufficient as a total philosophy. It is nevertheless true that the practical consequences of faith form an important commentary on the truth revealed. In this sense the doctrine of inspiration is subject to pragmatic test, and the history of the Church is characterized by its attitude toward the authority of the Bible.

The teaching that the Bible in its original writings was infallible, without error, and therefore authoritative has been a major factor in Christian theology, ethics, and the interpretation of experience. It is not too much to say that this one Christian dogma has been more determinative than any other in the detailed formulation of the Christian faith.

Pragmatic confirmation of Scriptural authority includes the practical influence of that authority on theology, the transforming power of an authoritative Bible in regeneration and sanctification, and the salutary effect of its recognition on the Church as a whole. Although it may be granted that the results of Scriptural authority are not in themselves absolute proof of its truth, they

179

do contribute to the judgment of its congruity to the total Christian point of view. The contrast of the contradictory and destructive force of disbelief to the beneficial effects of accepted authority in historic Christianity is evident. The concept of scriptural inerrancy and authority is an integral part of essential Christianity without which the whole disintegrates.

The major areas of pragmatic confirmation of scriptural authority are in bibliology as a whole, Christology, anthropology, soteriology, eschatology, and ethics. The infallibility of Scripture has established an absolute standard in both theology and ethics as well as providing the guidelines for interpretation and application of ethical truths in the total social and cultural complex. In addition to establishing moral standards and exerting moral influence, the doctrine of scriptural authority and infallibility has supported the revelation of God's program of regeneration and sanctification, which deal with the divine method and the grace for transformation of human character. In relation to spiritual experience, scriptural authority has provided an interpretive norm and has established the principle that experience must be evaluated by Scripture rather than that Scripture should be interpreted by experience, whether natural or supernatural. Because of its far-reaching practical character and vital relationship to every aspect of Christian faith and life, the doctrine of verbal and plenary inspiration has assumed the role of being the *sine qua non* of evangelical theology.

THE AUTHORITY OF VERBAL INSPIRATION

One of the most important pragmatic effects of inspiration is its support of scriptural authority. In accepting the doctrine of scriptural infallibility and divine inspiration, any Biblical scholar is automatically recognizing the objective authority of Scripture as the very Word of God. Augustine held that inspiration assured the inerrancy, authority, and incomprehensibility of Scripture.

David W. Kerr has summed up Augustine's attitude toward inspiration in these words, "If we add together the three factors which are bound up with Augustine's high view of inspiration, that is, inerrancy, authority and incomprehensibility, we shall quite readily see why he insists that one must approach the Bible with faith if he is to understand it at all. . . . The Bible is to be believed because it is authoritative; it is authoritative because it is inerrant; it is inerrant because it is inspired; it is inspired because holy men of old spake as they were moved by the Holy Ghost."[1] Whatever the degree of human participation in the writing of the Word of God, verbal and plenary inspiration asserts that every word of the Bible was written under infallible influence from God, and that the words therefore have the same authority as if God Himself had wielded the pen. In Scriptures which are directly dictated this is quite obvious.

Verbal and plenary inspiration, as understood by evangelicals today, is not synonymous with dictation, but allows for a degree of genuinely human activity. The resultant product, whether the outcome of historical research as in the case of Luke, the selection of correct records by a scribe reciting Old Testament history, the recording of spiritual experience as is typical of many Psalms, or the writing of prophecy dealing with future events is the infallible Word of God. Even though the degree of human participation may vary, the authority in every case is the same. Although human purposes are often revealed in the Scriptures and although these purposes spring naturally from human volition, the doctrine of inspiration presupposes a sovereign God who can work with the same degree of certainty through the human will as He can through natural law or through His own supernatural activity. The God of the Scriptures is in supreme control.

This concept of a sovereign God is in view when Isaiah quoted Jehovah as saying, "Declaring the end from the beginning, and from ancient times things that are not yet done; saying, My counsel shall stand, and I will do all my pleasure; calling a ravenous bird from the east, the man of my counsel from a far country; yea, I have spoken, I will also bring it to pass; I have purposed, I will also do it" (Isaiah 46:10, 11).

The doctrine of infallibility of Scripture extends to authority the absolute quality of being as true as God is true. Scripture, however, must be understood in its context and within the framework of both the divine and the human intent. Its ultimate meaning is subject to normal rules of interpretation and application, and facts and principles enunciated in the Bible, although absolute in their authority, are not necessarily universal in their application. The doctrine of verbal and plenary inspiration, however, assures the highest possible standard of truth and dismisses the question whether the Scripture is true, leaving only the question of its meaning and its reasonable implications. The doctrine of scriptural authority at one stroke minimizes the subjectivity and the relativity of human concepts, and introduces the reader of the Bible to a divine revelation given by a God who cannot lie.

Although it may be contended that the Bible could have authority apart from verbal and plenary inspiration, it is obvious that this authority would be subject to human judgment. The authority of Scripture apart from verbal and plenary inspiration would be no more than the congruity of scriptural truth with what seems normal in experience and rational in total philosophy. Scriptural authority could, therefore, be challenged by any reader as being incongruous either with other Scripture or with truth recognized on other principles. The authority of Scripture in this case would be transferred from the written word as inspired of God to its interpreter, and would be as fallible as human interpretation. Unquestionably the relationship of verbal inspiration to scriptural authority is the crux of all Christian theology and provides a principle which bifurcates all theological systems as resting either in divine inspiration or in human judgments.

SCRIPTURAL AUTHORITY IN BIBLIOLOGY

In bibliology, the theology of the Bible itself, the doctrine of scriptural infallibility stemming from verbal and plenary inspiration is the major determinative principle in establishing Biblical authority. Obviously a Bible which is infallible and given by inspiration of God is quite different from a Bible arising from human ingenuity and genius, even if influenced supernaturally to some degree. In such a bibliology, the absolute principle of infallibility is antithetical to whatever degree of fallibility is conceded by other views of inspiration.

In bibliology there is a sharp contrast between books considered canonical and noncanonical books. Inspiration, of course, extends only to those judged canonical, and no inspiration or infallibility is attributed to any other work, however nearly it may approximate scriptural truth. In Protestantism the canonicity of the sixty-six books of the Bible is sufficiently well established so that this is no longer an open question. In contemporary evangelicalism a denial of any of the canonical books is tantamount to questioning the doctrine of inspiration as it extends to others. Generally speaking, those who accept the verbal and plenary inspiration accept also the sixty-six books of the Bible and agree that inspiration extends equally to each of them, but no further.

Other theological concepts usually included in bibliology are also vitally affected by this doctrine. The living character of the Bible sometimes denominated as animation is directly related to the concept that the Bible is inspired of God. Its living character is dependent on the work of God which brought the Bible into being and set it apart from all other books.

It is in the realm of interpretation, however, that the doctrine of authority has its greatest practical effect. The interpreter, if the Bible is accepted as infallible, does not need to raise the question as to whether the Scriptures are true. He can therefore concentrate on the normal process of determining the true meaning of Scripture, and having found that true meaning can attribute to it the quality of divine authority and accuracy. Although interpretation necessarily has a human quality which introduces the possibility of error in understanding to the extent that interpretation is not in itself infallible, the fact that the materials being interpreted are inspired of God lends to the interpretation an authority which otherwise would be missing.

The process of interpretation of Scripture is more than merely a rational or experiential approach, for the Scriptures reveal that the Word of God can only be understood when one is taught by the Holy Spirit. This presupposes an epistemology in which the interpreter has insight into the real meaning of Scripture, springing from the fact that he is a believer who has been regenerated and indwelt by the Holy Spirit. That which a natural unregenerate man, however brilliant, could not understand, because "the things of the Spirit of God . . . are foolishness unto him" (I Corinthians 2:14), can only be known by the teaching ministry of the Holy Spirit, "because they are spiritually discerned." The inspiration of the Scripture, therefore, introduces a dramatically different kind of interpretation inasmuch as it recognizes the infallibility and supernatural character of the Scriptures themselves, as well as the supernatural process of understanding and interpreting the Scripture which involves the teaching ministry of the Holy Spirit. Although the process of interpretation is not completely exempt from the natural fallibility of human reason and reaction to divine revelation, it is significant that those who agree to the doctrine of the inerrancy of the Scriptures generally also agree on important fundamentals of theology which are plainly written in the Scriptures.

The doctrine of the inspiration of the Bible, although presenting truths in a timeless way, necessarily requires each passage to be understood within its context. The inspiration of the Bible does not relieve the interpreter of the responsibility for determining the proper limits of application of a given text. Proof texts cannot be taken from the Bible on the excuse that they are infallible and timeless, and made applicable to any situation which was not contemplated in the original divine and human intent when the Scriptures themselves were written. Hence, passages addressed to the unsaved must be understood in this context. Passages addressed to Christians should be understood as addressed to Christians. Promises given to Israel or to any other particular people should be examined in the light of this limited application. The promiscuous use of proof texts apart from proper contexts and understanding is all too prevalent in cults appealing to the Bible for their authority. The normal rules of interpretation must be applied to the Scriptures even if it be accepted that the Scriptures themselves are inerrant and a revelation of the eternal God.

The fact that the Bible is inspired of God supports a number of practical conclusions properly viewed as aspects of bibliology. One of these important aspects is the unity of the Bible. Although written by many human authors who came from varied backgrounds and who lived in different cultures and historic environments, the Bible is nevertheless one book, not sixty-six books. The unity of the Bible is demonstrated in the fact that it bears witness to one God, not many gods. The revelation of

God given in Genesis is integral to the revelation of God given in the other sixty-five books of the Scriptures.

The Scriptures have also historical continuity beginning with the creation of the world and of man, extending throughout the history of the race, and attaining fulfillment in the prophecy of future events. As the progress of Biblical history unfolds, it becomes a divine revelation of God's normative dealings with men under His government. The Old Testament, obviously incomplete with the close of Malachi, has its complement and capstone in the New Testament record of the incarnation, life, death, and resurrection of Christ, the proclamation of the grace and truth revealed through Christ, and in the prophetic climax of history as predicted in the New Testament.

The fact that the Bible has many human authors does not hinder the process of prediction and fulfillment of prophecy, nor does it hinder the progressive revelation of God where one writer adds new truth to that which a previous writer has recorded. Many great doctrines bind the sixty-six books of the Bible together, of which the most important is redemption in Jesus Christ. The supreme subject of the Scriptures is Christ. He is first mentioned as "the seed of the woman" in the garden of Eden, and there is a constantly unfolding revelation of Him, climaxing in the last book of the Bible.

The fact of the unity of the Bible is at once a result of verbal inspiration and its apologetic. It would be impossible to select from the thousands of books written in history any other group of sixty-six books which could be combined in such a unity as is found in the Scriptures.

The pragmatic effect of inspiration in the area of bibliology is seen also in the nature of the truth revealed. No other sacred book offers a world view which takes man from eternity to eternity with the comprehension, detail, and relevance to history such as the Bible provides. No other book plumbs greater depths of insight into timeless truth, or rises to loftier heights of description of the glory of God and His ineffable person. The truths of the Bible, whether viewed from the standpoint of history, ethics, human experience, or prophecy, have no rivals in all the religions of the world.

The truth of the Bible in its total presentation is infinitely superior to any of its competitors. Although the Bible has aroused the hostility of man because of its merciless disclosure of man's inadequacy in sin and its incisive puncturing of human pride and wisdom, the Scriptures have survived every attempt to destroy them, and stand in the twentieth century a monument to their own impregnability. While most ancient works have long since been lost and modern works soon vanish into oblivion, the Bible through the ages has had a continuity and a distribution equaled by no other literature of the world. All of these amazing qualities spring from the verbal and plenary inspiration of the Bible and the unique bibliology which results.

CHRISTOLOGY

The fact that Christology has been closely related to belief in scriptural inspiration is only natural because of the prominence of Christology in both the Old and New Testament. The importance of Christology, however, has been brought into focus by the attempt of both liberal and neo-orthodox interpreters of Scripture to attribute ultimate authority to Christ Himself rather than to the Scriptures. The theory accordingly has been advanced that while questions may be raised concerning the truth of the Scriptures in general as being somewhat contradictory to modern concept, the ultimate appeal must be to the person and teaching of Jesus Christ. Authority is therefore transferred from the written Word to the incarnate Word.

Such a procedure, however, ignores a most important fact; namely, that the knowledge of Christ is derived only from the written Scriptures. While there is plain evidence that the record concerning Christ is "His story," and has as much natural credence as any other sayings attributed to men who lived in the ancient world, the question of the reliability of the record is inseparable from the doctrine of inspiration itself.

Apart from the doctrine of inspiration, an interpreter of the sayings of Christ would be without a genuinely authoritative text. The teachings of Christ as they are presented in the Scriptures expressly deny the major premise of the point of view that Christ can be trusted, but that the Scriptures are fallible. Again and again in His teachings there are both direct statements and implications which assert the infallibility and divine origin of the Scriptures of the Old Testament and predict as well the inspiration of the New Testament. Christ denounced the Pharisees for "making void the word of God by your tradition, which ye have delivered" (Mark 7:13). In this passage he attributes to the Scriptures the quality of being the Word of God, which cannot lightly be disregarded. Again, Christ issued the pronouncement, "For verily I say unto you, Till heaven and earth pass away, one jot or one tittle shall in no wise pass away from the law, till all things be accomplished" (Matthew 5:18). He supported with His authority the most minute part of Scripture, namely the smallest letter of the Hebrew alphabet, referred to as a "jot," and the smallest part of a letter which could change its meaning, referred to as a "tittle." If the teachings of Christ are true, the Scriptures also must be inspired.

In discussing His passion with the disciples on the road to Emmaus, "beginning from Moses and from all the prophets, [Christ] interpreted to them in all the scriptures the things concerning himself" (Luke 24:27). He confirmed the accuracy of prophecy and the certainty of its fulfillment.

In the discussion of the rich man in Hades, Christ is recorded as saying, "If they hear not Moses and the prophets, neither will they be persuaded, if one rise from the dead" (Luke 16:31). Their refusal to hear Moses and the prophets is equated with a rejection of divine truth resulting in their failure to enter into salvation. Not only did Christ affirm the inspiration of the Old Testament, but also He anticipated the divine inspiration of the New. To His disciples He predicted that the Holy Spirit "shall teach you all things, and bring to your remembrance all that I said unto you" (John 14:26). He added further that "when he, the Spirit of truth, is come, he shall guide you into all the truth: for he shall not speak from himself; but what things soever he shall hear, these shall he speak: and he shall declare unto you the things that are to come. He shall glorify me: for he shall take of mine, and shall declare it unto you" (John 16: 13, 14).

In these numerous passages, Christ provides a complete and authoritative accreditation for the Bible as the Word of God. It is therefore impossible to evade the implication that if the teaching of Christ is accurate and without error then the Scriptures also are infallible. The integrity of the Scriptures and the integrity of the person of Christ are inseparable. It is for this reason that denial of the inspiration of the Scripture when carried to its logical conclusion has led historically to the denial of the person of Jesus Christ and the reduction of His deity in some measure below the infinite standard attributed to Him in the Scriptures. Conversely, those who accept the verbal and plenary inspiration of the Bible inevitably also accept the deity of Jesus Christ, and in modern times there is no considerable portion of the Church which denies the deity of Christ without denying also the inspiration of Scripture. It may be concluded that one of the important pragmatic effects of verbal and plenary inspiration with its corollary, authority, is that it leads one to the eternal Son of God who is the Lord of all life and the Saviour of all who believe.

ANTHROPOLOGY

Biblical anthropology, like other areas of theology, has largely been determined by acceptance or rejection of scriptural infallibility. Although the inspiration of the Bible has not completely resolved differences of opinion as reflected in the Calvinistic and Arminian views of man, most major questions are answered once the issue of scriptural infallibility is determined. In the Scriptures, man is presented in Genesis as well as elsewhere as the object of immediate creation. It is most significant that attempts to introduce a concept of theistic evolution have almost inevitably attended an ultimate departure from the doctrine of scriptural infallibility. Although technically a passage of Scripture can be regarded as an allegory and therefore nonhistorical or supra-historical without denying its infallibility, the introduction of nonhistorical or supra-historical interpretation of the Genesis narrative of creation is built upon a foundation which denies its infallibility and verbal inspiration. The reason for this is that the immediate creation of Adam and Eve is inextricably bound up with the total theology of the Bible, and is confirmed by many references outside of Genesis supporting the concept of immediate creation. Interpreters who have denied the historicity of Adam and Eve have usually been caught in the extension of the allegorical interpretation to later Scripture. Cain and

Abel, Noah and his family, and even Abraham are reduced to myths or allegorical tales instead of considering them as actual history. The effect of such an interpretation upon the total theology of Scripture colors not only anthropology with its doctrine of historic fall into sin, but also has tremendous ramifications affecting the doctrine of salvation and the meaning of Scripture far beyond the borders of the early chapters of Genesis.

Historically, the doctrine of authority has not settled all important questions regarding the origin of man. The problem of human antiquity and the length of the days of creation have been variously understood by those who without question have accepted the verbal and plenary inspiration of the Bible. The time of man's creation and the length of the creative process are not clearly delineated in the Bible. Some evangelicals have viewed the creation of Genesis 1 and 2 as a re-creation rather than the original creation of the physical universe. Although the total chronology cannot be determined from the Bible, the fact of the immediate creation of man and of the animals and plants after their kind is so closely related to the matter of verbal and plenary inspiration that almost automatically those who accept the Bible as authoritative also interpret the creation process literally.

What is true of the doctrine of origins as relating to man is also true of the Biblical analysis of human nature. The anthropology erected upon an infallible Bible inevitably pictures man as fallen into sin and needing divine grace and regeneration. The doctrine of the divine authority of Scripture is therefore seen to be determinative pragmatically in the major elements relating to anthropology, although not settling beyond dispute the details concerning the antiquity of man, and questions such as the divisions of his nature (dichotomy and trichotomy).

Soteriology

Since soteriology is one of the major themes of the Bible it is inevitable that its proper understanding should be vitally related to the matter of verbal and plenary inspiration. Combined in soteriology are the judgments formed previously in Christology and anthropology. On the one hand, soteriology presupposes a historic fall into sin on the part of Adam and Eve and the resultant depravity of man and need of divine grace and salvation. On the other hand, soteriology builds upon the person of Christ as absolute God and perfect man incarnate. Those who have held to the infallible inspiration of the Bible inevitably accept the eternity of Christ, His virgin birth, His complete deity, and His perfect humanity. The historic facts attributed to Him in the gospels and in other portions of Scripture are accepted at face value. The interpretation in the Bible of His acts in life, His death on the cross, and His bodily resurrection form the important structure of the doctrine of salvation and materially affect the particular doctrines which comprise the whole of soteriology.

As in the case of anthropology, the authority of the Bible does not determine all of the details of interpretation. Arminian interpreters in some instances accept the infallibility of the Bible without interpreting the Scriptures as teaching eternal security and related Calvinistic concepts. Although the doctrine of infallibility has not been completely determinative in the Calvinistic and Arminian concepts of soteriology, it is nevertheless true that the authority of the Bible has supported interpreting it as teaching substitutionary atonement and the supernatural and irrevocable character of divine regeneration.

It has been characteristic of theology that the rejection of the doctrine of substitutionary atonement ultimately leads to abandonment also of the doctrine of inspiration. In all major and important aspects of soteriology, the assumption of the doctrine of scriptural infallibility and authority has carried with it a heavy influence in the interpretation of the Scriptures themselves, with the result that those who accept scriptural authority have fewer problems of basic agreement in this important area of theology.

ESCHATOLOGY

In no field of theology is the matter of the authority of the Bible more important than in the area of prophecy. Although much prophecy has been fulfilled and has already demonstrated a marvelous accuracy in the Scriptures, it is obvious that unfulfilled prophecy must stand upon the bare Word of God. If the Bible is inspired infallibly such prophecies can be taken as prewritten history with all the accuracy and detail that history itself could afford. On the other hand, if the Bible is not infallible, then all prophecy is suspect and nothing can be certain until it is fulfilled.

The field of eschatology has been an important apologetic for the infallibility of Scripture. In spite of attempts to postdate prophetic books such as Daniel with the hope of dating the books after the events predicted, such a process completely fails in connection with Christological prophecies which obviously were fulfilled after the completion of the Old Testament. The numerous prophecies which were fulfilled in the birth, life, death and resurrection of Christ not only served to link the doctrine of Christ with the doctrine of inspiration, but also illustrate the pragmatic result of inspiration in the field of eschatology. If it is true, as has been estimated, that half of the prophecies of Scripture have already been fulfilled with amazing literalness, the authority and infallibility of Scripture have the practical effect of giving certitude to prophecies yet to be fulfilled.

The acceptance of the authority of Scripture normally carries with it an appreciation of the accuracy of great themes of prophecy. Among the most important are prophecies relating to the person and work of Christ which are found extensively in both the Old and New Testament. Prominent also are prophecies relating to the nation of Israel which form such a large portion of the Old Testament and to which the New Testament contributes additional light. An amazing amount of material is also provided in the Scriptures concerning the program of God for the nations of the world. The prophet Daniel reveals the outline with his four great world empires, and other prophets add many details. Transcending the distinction between Israel and the Gentiles are prophecies relating to the saints of all ages that predict their ultimate triumph, their resurrection or translation, and their eternal bliss in the city of God, the new Jerusalem. Practically all of these details of prophecy hang upon the question of the authority of the Scriptures, and those who deny scriptural infallibility also tend to ignore or deny the prophetic teaching in these major areas.

Authoritative Ethics

Except for radical critics who have denounced the ethics of the Old Testament, there has been general recognition of the beneficial moral influence of Scripture. The evidence is massive that wherever the Bible has been preached and heeded there has been a corresponding influence which has raised men from the lowest depths of moral degradation to the heights of nobility of purpose and purity of life. No savage tribe or even a relatively cultured society like that of ancient Greece has ever carried the label of "Puritan," such as was given to the early colonists of America. Although moral standards have varied in the heathen world, no civilization has achieved the nobility and morality of a Christian society dominated by Christian faith and ethics.

The relevance of authority to the trustworthiness of the Bible and its practical effect on those to whom it is preached is brought out by Loraine Boettner: "But how different is our attitude toward it when we approach it as the very word of God, an inspired, infallible rule of faith and practice! How readily we accept its statements of fact and bow before its enunciations of duty! How instinctively we tremble before its threatenings, and rest upon its promises! As we proclaim the Word of God from the pulpit, or in the classroom; as we attempt to give comfort at some bed of sickness, or in a bereaved home; or as we see our fellow men struggling against temptation or weighted down with care, and would give them encouragement and hope for this world and the next, how thankful we then are for a fully trustworthy Bible! In such cases we want to know that we have not merely something which is probable or plausible, but something which is sure."[2]

Unquestionably, the Bible, even if viewed as a human instrument apart from verbal and plenary inspiration, would have a salutary effect upon any individual or society which paid serious heed to its instruction. If the infallibility of the Bible should remain unrecognized, however, the reader of Scripture no longer could take the dictums of the Bible as authoritative and would need to submit the ethics of Scripture to the searching subjective question of whether the standards set forth in the Scriptures are after all worthy of universal recognition. Ultimately the interpreter of Scripture who denies its authority is thrown back upon one or more principles of non-Christian ethics, and inevitably adopts a standard of ethics which is subjective and relative, and which lacks the element of absolute divine authority.

The doctrine of scriptural authority gives to the moral precepts of the Bible the quality of being the expressed will of God. The Scriptures become a divine standard rather than a human expedient and their moral precepts are undergirded by the proclamation, "Thus saith the Lord." The expositor of the Word of God can depend on the scriptural authority of His message.

The relevance of authority to effective expository preaching has been summarized by R. B. Kuyper: "But for him who is convinced that the Bible is 'God-breathed' in all its parts and that for this very reason the parts together constitute a perfectly harmonious whole, there is no better method of preaching than this. Because he is convinced that every part of the Bible is the Word of God, he would analyze. Because he is convinced that the whole Bible is the Word of God, he would synthesize. The combination of correct scriptural analysis and sound scriptural synthesis insures scriptural preaching *par excellence*."[3]

Scriptural revelation as it relates to ethics is not without its serious problems. The Scriptures make no effort to varnish the characters portrayed in the Bible with an unnatural and unrealistic moral purity. Even principal characters such as Noah, Moses, and David are portrayed for what they were, men of natural passions who in part at least had been subdued by the grace of God so that they could be instruments to accomplish the will of God. Scripture does not hide the fact that the moral precepts of the Bible are frequently disregarded, and attained to perfection by no one except the Lord Jesus Christ. This realistic approach, however, actually supports the high standard of Biblical ethics, because the reader is constantly reminded of the gulf which lies between the perfection of divine morality as revealed in the holiness of God and the imperfection of the creature born in sin, and able only in partial measure to rise above his natural heritage even by the grace of God.

Many critics have been outspoken in their denunciation of Old Testament ethics. The destruction of entire cities and nations as commanded by God, including men, women, and children, the tolerance of slavery and warfare, and lack of express condemnation of other attitudes and actions that seem incongruous with a God who is holy, just, and good, are itemized with enthusiasm by those who find the Old Testament far below a proper standard of ethics. That there are problems in this area no one will deny, but the chief problem arises in the lack of human comprehension of divine righteousness and of the motivation which is evident in divine commands to exterminate wicked people whom God has tolerated for many generations. In this area and in others, the Scriptures are their own defense; for when the people of Israel neglected to carry out God's commands to exterminate depraved civilizations which they found in the Promised Land, it resulted inevitably in their own moral downfall. This demonstrated that even the acts of judgment upon wicked people were a reflection of the innate goodness of God, which prompted destruction of the heathen, that the people of God might be preserved a nation peculiar and different from their wicked neighbors.

Ultimately the problem in radical criticism of Old Testament ethics is the failure to comprehend that a God of love is also a God of infinite righteousness. Instead of raising questions concerning the compatibility of divine acts of judgment with God's love and grace, the question may well be asked how a holy God could tolerate both Gentiles and Israelites who so completely failed to comprehend His holiness and to correspond at least partially to the divine standards. The fact remains that God's righteous wrath on the wicked is part of His ethical revelation and has served to warn them as well as to encourage the righteous down through the centuries. The reading of both the Old and New Testament has exercised a salutary ethical effect upon all who have carefully observed its precepts.

History has recorded numerous illustrations of men and women who through reading of the Scriptures and hearing the Word of God preached have had their lives radically altered. No other so-called world religion has had the moral impact of Christianity and the inherent ability to transform men from the lowest depraved estate to men of noble character. This has been evidenced in countless missionary situations where raw savages have been transformed into civilized and law-abiding Christians within one generation. In civilized lands the same amazing power has repeatedly taken men of moral degradation, victims of drink and of every immorality, and made them respectable representatives of Christian character.

Dr. R. A. Torrey used to tell the story of two infidels who were shipwrecked on a South Sea island. Afraid of cannibals who inhabited the area, they lived in fear and ventured forth from hiding places only after dark. After many days they were finally reconciled to the necessity of contact with the people on the island if they were to be rescued. Approaching a village they saw in the distance a church spire. They greeted the sight with great enthusiasm, reasoning correctly that if there was a church in the village they need not fear the natives. Their involuntary recognition of the transforming effect of the Gospel upon those who had lived in savage cannibalism bears its own witness to the transforming power which can make saints out of savages.

The tremendous moral influence of scriptural ethics with its corresponding Gospel of grace is not without its contradictions. Many in history who have professed to follow Christ whether in the nation of Israel or in the Church have often failed to be true examples of Biblical ethics. The Church has been guilty of heinous crimes in the name of religion, including the persecution of minority groups and the martyrdom of those who have differed in theology. It is obvious that the ethics of the Bible are not automatically fulfilled, and that readers of Scripture are not invariably transformed by its precepts.

The fault, however, lies not in the ethics of the Bible, but in failure to make any realistic attempt to conform to the standard of divine holiness because of misunderstanding and misapplication. In spite of these glosses upon pragmatic Christian testimony to the ethics of Scripture, the contrast between the morality of faith and unbelief is all too evident. If one hundred men fully dedicated to the principles of Biblical ethics could be compared with one hundred men fully dedicated to the principle of unbelief in the Scripture, the contrasting morality of faith versus unbelief would stand in bold relief. Wherever Biblical ethics have been observed, there have been honesty, integrity, elevation of women to respectable status, kindness, self-sacrifice, deliverance from gross sin, and manifestation of all the other graces which characterize a life dominated by the Holy Spirit. Such influences are most evident among those who recognize the infallibility of Scripture and accept the Bible as the authoritative Word of God.

AUTHORITATIVE INTERPRETATION OF REVELATORY EXPERIENCE

The Church of the mid-twentieth century has been accurately described as the Church of crisis theology and existential philosophy. The advance of religious liberalism which characterized the last quarter of the nineteenth century and the opening of the twentieth was arrested by the soul-searching experience of World War I. The hard facts of man's depravity and the evidence that scientific improvement did not bring regeneration of society tended to halt the unrealistic trends in both theology and philosophy and introduced a new realism. Man after all needed more than materialistic psychology and philosophy — he needed a supernatural God.

This supernatural ingredient introduced by the penetrating exposition of the *Epistle to the Romans* by Karl Barth struck liberalism in its naturalistic vitals. Here was one using liberal terminology but renouncing a naturalistic approach to life as totally inadequate. Reintroduced was the supernatural element and the thesis that the infinite God can, in spite of all arguments to the contrary, communicate to finite man experientially.

The experiential crisis of the immediate divine revelation which Karl Barth propounded was far short of Biblical orthodoxy, although it was soon called neo-orthodoxy because of its supernaturalism. The new definition of revelation bypassed the whole question of scriptural infallibility and the authority of the written Word, and transferred the divine work of revelation from the written Word historically oriented to the immediate subjective experience of the individual who sensed a revelation from God regardless of its means. It was a revelation of the moment, detached from the history of the past as well as from prophecy of the future, and was existentialism in theological form.

Although dogmatic and irrational rather than supported by history and fact, the new approach purported at least to provide a sure word from God. Here was a divine touch in human personality without facing all of the problems of higher and lower criticism, problems of truth or error in Scripture, and the clamor of various creeds. Each individual was the captain of his own theology. His own subjective experience, supposedly supernatural and divine in its origination, could satisfy the individual that he had captured his moment of truth and was thereby delivered from the finite limitations of human reason.

The history of crisis theology has already demonstrated, however, that it lacks a corrective norm. Adherents have galloped in every direction theologically and have ended in theologies mutually contradictory, not only in nonessentials but in fundamentals. Unitarians, Trinitarians, outspoken liberals, as well as confused conservatives have alike embraced the theory, but lacking a norm each has developed his own point of view. The weakness of the new theology lay in the fact that it was based upon individual experience. The conflicting aspects of the supposed supernatural element of divine revelatory experience in different individuals seemingly could not originate from the God of the Bible. The supernaturalism of the crisis experience was too often from a God of man's creation rather than a God who is the Creator of man.

The contrast between the new experiential theology, whatever its particular tenets, and the theology springing from an authoritative Bible written in historic context is becoming increasingly evident with each passing year. Again the history of interpretation supports the pragmatic confirmation of scriptural authority. Only an objective standard such as a written word, inherently infallible, and a theology consistent with this total revelation can produce a proper basis for interpretation of spiritual experience.

As illustrated in false mysticism and the overemphasis on experience which has characterized certain periods of church history, the meaning of spiritual experience must always be subject to the objective revelation of the Word of God. Nothing can be added to normative truth which is already not inherent in the written Word. The teaching ministry of the Holy Spirit in interpreting the Bible, and the guidance of the Holy Spirit as Biblical truths are applied to life are the nearest approach to infallibility in experience which it is possible for mortal man to achieve. Always the principle remains that interpretation of the Bible and guidance and decision are no more accurate than their conformity to the objective written Word of God. The norm inevitably must be the Scriptures, not the individual experience.

The pragmatic influence of verbal and plenary inspiration accordingly stands infinitely superior to any of its modern substitutes. In relation to reason there is pragmatic confirmation that the Bible is supra-rational, for no man knows enough to contradict the teachings of the Bible. In relation to experience, whether psychological or a product of supernatural influence of the Holy Spirit, only the Scriptures can provide a sure standard by which that experience can be interpreted, evaluated, and understood. While the subjective quality of Christian experience can never be eliminated and the infinite variety of human reaction to the Word of God is inevitable, only a Bible infallible in its original writings can produce a stable theology as well as a consistent life. Whether in theology, ethics, prophecy, or world view, only the Scriptures can provide the necessary insight, information, and guidelines to provide the test for all human judgments.

In the twentieth century as in all preceding periods of human history, the written Word of God stands supreme as the ultimate test of human faith and behavior and the basis on which God Himself will evaluate the world and its individuals. Towering over the wrecks of time, the Word of God will also survive all its temporal competitors. As Christ Himself said, "Heaven and earth shall pass away, but my words shall not pass away" (Matthew 24:35). Present as well as future experiences of the saints provide pragmatic confirmation of the authority and infallibility of the Scriptures.

THE RELEVANCE OF SCRIPTURE TODAY

John Warwick Montgomery

John Warwick Montgomery

John Warwick Montgomery is Professor and Acting Chairman of the Division of Church History in Trinity Evangelical Divinity School, Bannockburn, Deerfield, Illinois. He is the author of *The Shape of the Past, A Seventeenth Century View of European Libraries, Crisis in Lutheran Theology,* and *The 'Is God Dead?' Controversy.* He holds the degrees of Ph.D. from the University of Chicago, and the Th.D. from the University of Strasbourg.

Chapter X

THE RELEVANCE OF
SCRIPTURE TODAY

THEOLOGY, no less than secular fields of endeavor, is subject to changing fashions in terminology. A semanticist could easily plot the course of twentieth century Protestant thought by analyzing the life cycle of in-group jargon such as "existential encounter" and "eschatological moment." Currently, no expression is quite as popular theologically as the word "relevance." On every hand — in book, magazine article, and sermon — appears the statement that the Christian faith and its Bible must be "made relevant to modern man." The lengths to which contemporary churchmen are going in the quest for "relevance" seem endless; the March 10, 1967, issue of *Time* describes, under the appropriate rubric, "Secular Sermons," an Emory University chaplain who projected illustrations from *Playboy* onto the chancel wall as a backdrop for his Sunday sermon, and a Birmingham, Michigan, clergyman who passed out lumps of clay and cardboard to his congregation so that they could sculpture themselves.

Even within the Protestant theological establishment, the cult of relevance is beginning to call forth satire and parody — a sure sign that its coinage is in process of devaluation. Thus Robert McAfee Brown, in a chapter of his *Collected Writings of St. Hereticus* (1964), titled, "Making the Bible Relevant: Biblical Needs and How to Meet Them," offers a "relevant" retelling of the Easter story:

But on the first day of the week, toward dawn, they arose
and went to the garden in convertibles, ranch wagons, and
Corvettes, wearing on their persons the spices they had prepared for the occasion. And behold, as the sun burst forth
there was a great blast from four trumpets, drawn from the
local high school marching band. And at the blast of the
trumpets, an Easter bunny, wondrous large, stood before
them. His appearance was like lightning, and his fur was
white as snow. And he did carry a sign affixed to his hat
bearing the words, "Courtesy of Jones's Department
Store. . . ."

Brown notes, quite properly, that his contemporary "scripture
lesson" is "sober and straightforward reporting of the various
strata of twentieth-century religious insight." This is in point of
fact the very difficulty in theologies of "relevance": they take
modern man as normative and endeavor to reconstruct Christianity and the Bible in his cultural image. As written elsewhere,
modern theology has engaged in "an impossible attempt to make
the Christian message fit the demands of the unregenerate man."[1]

It is the firm conviction of this writer that the Bible does not
need to be "made relevant" to twentieth-century man, any
more than it needed to be made relevant to fifth- or seventeenth-
century man. Holy Scripture, as the utterance of the living
God, is by its very nature the most relevant Word ever spoken.
When Charles Spurgeon was asked by a feverish young man,
"Dr. Spurgeon, how can I defend the Bible?" the great expositor
replied: "How would you defend a lion? Let it out of its cage and
it will defend itself!" Persuaded by the testimony of Scripture
itself that God's Word never returns void (Isaiah 55:11) but is
"living, and active, and sharper than any two-edged sword"
(Hebrews 4:12), the present essay will endeavor to demonstrate
that irrelevance exists not where a fully authoritative Scripture is
proclaimed, but where it is denied, and that in this age as in
ages past the Bible meets the human situation in maximum
relevance and power.

THE BIBLE'S RELEVANCE IN THE PAST

As background for any analysis of the Bible in relation to
contemporary life, one does well to note the testimonies to its

relevance in former times. A common failing of men in every era is their naive belief that their own time constitutes a qualitatively different situation from all others, thereby rendering the Biblical Word somehow irrelevant for them. In actuality, as Reinhold Niebuhr said in another connection, "the fabric of history is woven upon one loom."[2] Every period of history has had its special problems, but they are no different qualitatively from those of other eras, for man remains man. Throughout the centuries, the testimonies of those who have allowed the Biblical message free rein in their lives show a remarkable similarity; they well illustrate that, in spite of changing cultural conditions, man remains a sinner in desperate need of the Word of life. Consider a few typical examples.

In the fourth century Chrysostom voiced the common conviction of patristic Christianity as to the excellence of Holy Scripture:

> Yea, rather the reading of the divine Scriptures is not a meadow only, but a paradise; for the flowers here have not a mere fragrance only, but fruit too, capable of nourishing the soul. Assuredly, then, we ought not hastily to pass by even those sentences of Scripture which are thought to be plain; for these also have proceeded from the grace of the Spirit: but this grace is never small nor mean, but great and admirable, and worthy the munificence of the giver; for pearls too, take their price, not from the size of the substance, but from the beauty of it. Even so is it with the reading of the divine Scriptures; for worldly instruction rolls forth its trifles in abundance, and deluges its hearers with a torrent of vain babblings, but dismisses them empty-handed, and without having gathered any profit, great or small.

Twelve centuries later the same reverence for the Biblical Word infused the life and thought of the Reformers. Here are only a few of the remarks made by Luther concerning the Bible:

> No book, teaching, or word is able to comfort in troubles, fear, misery, death, yea, in the midst of devils and in hell, except this book, which teaches us God's Word and in which God Himself speaks with us as a man speaks with his friend.

> No book but Holy Scripture can comfort us. It alone has the title St. Paul gives it: "the book of comfort" [Romans 15:4]. It can support the soul in all tribulations so that it does not give way to despair but keeps on hoping; for the soul appre-

hends the Word of God, in which it learns His gracious
will, to which it firmly clings, and thus remains unshaken
in life and death. But the man who does not know the will
of God must doubt; for he does not know what his relation
to God really is.

The Bible is the proper book for men. There the truth is
distinguished from error far more clearly than anywhere
else, and one finds something new in it every day. For
twenty-eight years, since I became a doctor, I have now constantly read and preached the Bible; and yet I have not
exhausted it but find something new in it every day.

Well after the onset of the modern secular era, the nineteenth-
century poet Heinrich Heine could still write of the Holy Scriptures:

What a Book! Vast and wide as the world, rooted in the
abysses of Creation, and towering up behind the blue secrets
of heaven! Sunrise and sunset, promise and fulfillment, birth
and death, the whole drama of humanity, all in this Book!

A few years after those lines were penned, Abraham Lincoln
addressed a letter to a Negro organization, in which, after discussing the issue of freedom ("it has always been a sentiment
with me that all mankind should be free"), he spoke of the
source of his religious and moral convictions:

In regard to this Great Book, I have but to say, it is the
best gift God has given to man. All the good the Saviour
gave to the world was communicated through this book. But
for it we could not know right from wrong. All things most
desirable for man's welfare, here and hereafter, are to be
found portrayed in it.

Testimonies of this kind to the relevance of the scriptural
Word through the ages could be multiplied virtually without
limit. The Bible, by virtue of its eternal authorship, has acted as
the most civilizing, radically transforming, and revolutionary
piece of literature in every age and clime where it has pene-
trated.

At best such considerations would reduce the parochial ar-
rogance of the modern man who assumes that the Scriptures
have always been more or less irrelevant to basic human needs.

But the marshalling of evidence for the Bible's impact on pre-twentieth century life would still leave the haunting question: Is the Bible relevant *today* — in the philosophical, religious, and cultural climate that will usher in century twenty-one? Can a fully authoritative Scripture, as attested by historic evangelical Christianity, speak as clearly to the needs of the present and the future as it evidently did to the needs of the past?

THE RELEVANCE OF SCRIPTURE IN TODAY'S PHILOSOPHICAL CLIMATE

The great Anglican divine E. A. Litton emphasized the unanimity of all branches of the Christian church in regard to the plenary inspiration of the Bible: "If there ever was a general consent of the Church Catholic on any question, it exists on this. East and West, from the earliest to the latest times, concurred in assigning to Scripture a pre-eminence which consisted in its being — as no other collection of writings is — the Word of God."[3] For classical Protestant theology, the Bible in its entirety is a message introduced by the eternal God into the human situation, and is therefore totally veracious both in its facts (its descriptive content) and in its values (its normative content). Moreover, having God as its author, Scripture is a clear book whose teachings can be objectively determined through the study and comparison of one portion of the Bible with another. When the objective truths of God's Word — and particularly the factual reality of Christ's death for man's sin and resurrection for his justification — are brought to bear on human life, they have the power to transform existence totally: "If any man is in Christ," declares the Apostle, "he is a new creature: the old things are passed away; behold, they are become new" (II Corinthians 5:17).

In a striking number of ways, this high view of Biblical authority maintained by orthodox Protestantism can establish ideological links with the latest and most fruitful advances in contemporary philosophical thought. Orthodox Christians of the nineteenth and early twentieth centuries experienced difficulties in resisting the ideological climate of their day, for the nineteenth century was characterized by a philosophical idealism such as that of Hegel and Bradley that confidently endeavored to set forth absolute truth apart from revelation. When these endeavors hopelessly failed, twentieth-century existentialism

(Heidegger, Sartre) gave up in principle the search for absolutes and substituted for objective truth and value a subjective relativism in which the individual determines the nature of his world through his own decisions. The nineteenth century tried to reach God through human reason, and the early twentieth century, having failed in constructing this Tower of Babel and finding its language confused, gave up all hope of eternal truth, and saw no other recourse than to make a philosophy of life out of the hopelessness of a confused existence. Both idealism and existentialism had been right and wrong simultaneously: idealism was right in believing that man desperately needed an absolute Word, but wrong in thinking that man could attain it by pulling himself to heaven by his own ideological bootstraps; existentialism was right in recognizing man's inability to arrive at absolute truth and value through his philosophical efforts, but wrong in giving up all hope of an eternal Word. The most recent developments in philosophical thinking point the way beyond this impasse and offer powerful testimony to the continuing relevance of the orthodox doctrine of Biblical authority.

At the root of the new look in twentieth-century philosophy is Ludwig Wittgenstein (1889-1951), a strange, eccentric, passionate seeker after philosophical integrity who combined mathematical-logical genius with intense mysticism. Says Justus Hartnack and he does not exaggerate — "Wittgenstein holds the key to modern philosophical activity."[4] In his remarkable *Tractatus Logico-Philosophicus*, Wittgenstein effectively argued that "the sense of the world must lie outside the world";[5] that is, man never has sufficient perspective from within the world situation to build an eternal structure of truth and value. Absolute truth and eternal value, if they exist at all, must take their origin from outside the flux of the human situation.

This insight has revolutionized all branches of philosophy and has dealt a virtual death blow to metaphysical idealism. Consider the realms of philosophy of history and ethics. The grandiose nineteenth- and early twentieth-century attempts (Hegel, Spengler, *et al.*) to construct universally valid interpretations of history apart from revelation are now seen to be impossible in principle; the philosopher simply cannot gain the perspective outside the world needed to explain the human drama.[6] As

Arthur C. Danto has shown, following in Wittgenstein's foot-
steps, the only "substantive philosophy of history" which is logically possible would be in reality *prophetic*: "It involves speaking
in a prophetic vein, i.e. describing the present in the light of
things which have not as yet happened ('Unto you a Saviour
is born')."[7]

Likewise in the realm of ethics, G. E. Moore, who considered
Wittgenstein his best student and who, with Bertrand Russell,
examined him for his doctorate, labeled as the "naturalistic
fallacy" any attempt to define "goodness" absolutely in the human sphere — particularly the attempt to create an absolute value
system simply on the basis of what people do.[8] More recently,
Kurt Baier, one of the foremost ethical thinkers to benefit from
Wittgensteinian insights, has admitted that from within the
human situation ethical values can never rise above the societal
level: "Outside society, the very distinction between right and
wrong vanishes."[9] Human beings, in other words, are incapable
of reaching absolute ethical norms by unaided reason; their ethic
will always reflect their stance in society. As Wittgenstein put it
in the *Tractatus*: "If there is any value that does have value, it
must lie outside the whole sphere of what happens and is the
case. . . . Ethics is transcendental" (6.41-6.421).[5]

The plain consequence is that the only possible answer to
modern man's quest for the ultimate meaning of history and for
an absolute ethical standard would have to lie in a revelation
from outside the world. If such a revelation does not exist, man
will of logical (not merely practical) necessity remain forever
bound to his cultural relativities, forever ignorant of life's meaning. But if such a revelation should exist, it would explode the
world — turn it, as men said the early Christians did, upside
down (Acts 17:6). Wittgenstein himself understood this very
clearly, as one sees from the following passage in the only
popular lecture he is known to have composed (the text remained
unpublished until its appearance in the January, 1965, *Philosophical Review*):

> And now I must say that if I contemplate what Ethics really
> would have to be if there were such a science, this result
> seems to me quite obvious. It seems to me obvious that
> nothing we could ever think or say should be *the* thing.

> That we cannot write a scientific book, the subject matter
> of which could be intrinsically sublime and above all other
> subject matters. I can only describe my feeling by the meta-
> phor, that, if a man could write a book on Ethics which
> really was a book on Ethics, this book would, with an ex-
> plosion, destroy all the other books in the world.[10]

It is the conviction of orthodox Christianity that in Holy Scripture just such a book exists: a Book "intrinsically sublime and
above all other subject matters" because its Author is the transcendent Lord God, who is unconditioned by the human predicament that corrupts even our best attempts to find life's meaning,
and who alone knows and is Absolute Truth.

But is the Bible the revelation Christians claim it is? Has it the
power to explode the world of human speculation? Sad to say,
neither Wittgenstein himself nor the analytical philosophy movement that stems from his work has seriously investigated the
question.[11] In Wittgenstein's personal life, one sees only the
profound and pathetic longings of one who recognized man's
overwhelming need for a Word from God but did not think any
avenue existed for its transmission; as his biographer Malcolm
described it: "Often as we walked together he would stop and
exclaim 'Oh, my God!', looking at me almost piteously, as if im-
ploring a divine intervention in human events."[12] But the
analytical philosophy movement — Wittgenstein's continuing leg-
acy — has provided the tools by which early twentieth-century
existential skepticism toward objective Biblical truth can be effectively countered, and the fact of "divine intervention" through
Scripture meaningfully proclaimed.

Characteristic of existential modes of thinking is Wilhelm
Dilthey's historical relativism. Dilthey argued that the historian
is never able to obtain a genuinely objective view of the past, for
his own subjectivity inevitably enters into his investigations of
earlier times. This viewpoint has been picked up by theological
existentialists such as radical New Testament critic and demy-
thologizer Rudolf Bultmann ("always in your present lies the
meaning in history"), by post-Bultmannians such as Heinrich Ott
("the objective mode of knowledge is entirely inappropriate to
historical reality because there are no such things as objectively
verifiable facts"), and by death-of-God theologians such as

Thomas J. J. Altizer who, on the basis of his belief that objective knowledge of the past is impossible, freely creates a "hidden Christ" in terms of his own present experience.

The insights of Wittgenstein-inspired analytical philosophy have done much to show the fallacy in this kind of approach to historical reality and to the literary products of the past. Summarizing the results, J. W. N. Watkins notes that, over against the Dilthey tradition, analytical work by such philosophers as Ryle "dispels the old presumption . . . that to understand Genghis Khan the historian must be someone very like Genghis Khan."[13] One can most definitely arrive at an objective knowledge of a Genghis Khan — or of a Moses or of Jesus Christ! The most recent and important collection of papers reflecting an analytical approach to historiography is William H. Dray's *Philosophical Analysis and History* (New York: Harper, 1966); the essays by C. G. Hempel and J. A. Passmore are especially devastating to the Dilthey-existential variety of historical skepticism. Hempel's closely reasoned paper on "Explanation in Science and in History" demonstrates "the methodological unity of all empirical science," i.e., the common ground between scientific and historical investigations. Passmore, in his essay on "The Objectivity of History," effectively argues in the same vein that skepticism toward history will necessarily involve one in skepticism both toward science and toward one's present experience, resulting in total solipsism. He concludes: "If we mean by 'science' the attempt to find out what really happens, then history is a science. It demands the same kind of dedication, the same ruthlessness, the same passion for exactness, as physics." Comparable realization in the literary field that objectivity of interpretation is possible can be seen in the work of the "neo-Aristotelians" such as Elder Olson, who shows that existential blendings of literary texts with their interpreters have produced "an endless succession of free improvisations" instead of an objective understanding of the great literary products of the past.[14] The Biblical implications of this recovery of confidence in historical and literary objectivity are no less than revolutionary. The orthodox Christian claim that Scripture is objectively true historical revelation, capable of yielding a clear message to all who without prejudice study its literary content, must now be taken with utmost seriousness.

The analytical philosophy movement has provided still another inestimable boon for evangelicals concerned to maintain the classic view of Biblical truth. Analytical philosophers have had much to say about "verifiability" and "meaningfulness"; they stress that truth-claims which are in principle unable to be confirmed or disconfirmed have no meaningful content. Philosopher Paul Edwards makes this point well in his critique of Tillich's theology:

> We normally regard as empty, as devoid of (cognitive) meaning or content a sentence which, while pretending to assert something, is on further examination found to be compatible with any state of affairs. If, for example, I say "Bomba is going to wear a red tie tonight" and if I do not withdraw my statement even. if he shows up wearing a brown or a black or a grey tie, and if it further becomes clear that I will not consider my statement refuted even if Bomba wears no tie at all and in fact that I will consider it "true," no matter what happens anywhere, then it would be generally agreed that I have really said nothing at all.[15]

Tillich and other contemporary theologians much influenced by existentialist modes of thought have been particularly prone to make religious statements that, being "compatible with any state of affairs" and totally without the possibility of confirmation or disconfirmation, are really meaningless. The attitudes toward Scripture taken by dialectic theologians such as Barth and by existential theologians such as Bultmann and his disciples precisely fit this category. For example, they affirm that the Bible, though an erroneous book, is revelatory because "God encounters us there" (Barth) or because "self-understanding" occurs in contact with it (Bultmann) or because "the text interprets us."[16] These subjectivistic approaches to Biblical inspiration are now revealed as hopelessly weak; they are in fact technically meaningless, for they are still maintained by the modern theologian regardless of the errors he purports to find in Scripture and regardless of the impossibility of testing subjective experience.

The orthodox Christianity of the Reformers and of the evangelical divines has never fallen into this pit; orthodoxy has consistently affirmed that the dynamic effect of Scripture on man's personal life occurs because Scripture is in fact objectively true. Personal truth is grounded in objective truth. Historic Chris-

tianity has always maintained a meaningful doctrine of inspiration which rests the case for the Bible's subjective validity on its
de facto objective truthfulness. By a very precise and con-
firmable argument (the historical reliability of the New Testament documents *qua* documents; the demonstrable deity of
Christ in those records; Christ's stamp of approval on the Old
Testament and His promise of identical, Spirit-led remembrance
of His Word among the apostles under whose aegis the New
Testament would be written), evangelical Christians offer to the
world today the only meaningful revelation-claim for the truth of
Holy Scripture.

Today, as never before, philosophical thought manifests a passion for objective, empirical truth, and the ordinary-language
philosophers, whose work stems from Wittgenstein's *Philosophical
Investigations*, are stressing the importance of verbal expression in
conveying truth. Evangelicals of the second half of the twentieth
century have an unparalleled opportunity to affirm the philosophical relevance of their high view of Scripture. The "divine intervention" for which Wittgenstein longed can with confidence be
offered to modern man in the totally veracious, inscripturated
Word of God.

THE RELEVANCE OF SCRIPTURE FOR THE CURRENT THEOLOGICAL SITUATION

Protestant theology in the 1960's is characterized above all by
the God-is-dead phenomenon. Though this movement, as represented particularly by Thomas J. J. Altizer and William Hamilton,
has inherent instabilities which will doubtless shorten its ideological life, one must not underestimate its importance. The death-
of-God phenomenon reflects the increasing secularization of our
time, which will certainly go on whether or not its advocates
retain their popularity; and, even more significantly, the God-is-
dead movement demonstrates the consequences of the weak view
of Holy Scripture that has prevailed in Protestant theology since
the advent of rationalistic Biblical criticism. By noting the con-
nections between God-is-dead thinking and destructive criticism
of Holy Writ, one can see quite plainly how evangelical Christianity's belief in a totally authoritative Word has maximum
relevance in a time of general theological collapse.

In a paper delivered at a program on radical theology sponsored by the University of Michigan's Office of Religious Affairs (October 28, 1966), William Hamilton unwittingly provided a laboratory example of how the demise of one's bibliology results in the demise of one's God. In answering the question, "Can you really maintain a loyalty to Jesus without a loyalty to God?" he said:

> Professor Altizer solves the problem more readily than I by his apocalyptic definition of Jesus, more Blakean than biblical, as the one who is born out of God's death. I am not yet ready to give up *sola scriptura* [!], and thus my answer must be more complex and tentative. . . . Early in the nineteenth century, we had to face, under the early impact of historical criticism, both that Jesus was firmly committed to demon-possession as the meaning of mental and physical illness, and that we were not so committed and needn't be. But obedience to Jesus was not destroyed. Later, at the time of Darwinian controversy, we had to face another instance of Jesus' full participation in the thought-forms of his day — the three-story, primitive cosmology. But we do not go to the Bible for science, we were rightly told, and obedience to Jesus was not hurt. At the close of the century we had to face an even more disturbing fact — the fact brought before us by Weiss and Schweitzer that Jesus was completely committed to the apocalyptic views of the Judaism of his day. . . . If Jesus' demonology and cosmology and eschatology were taken as first-century views, appropriate then, not so now, needing reinterpretation and understanding but not literal assent, what is inherently different about Jesus' *theology?*[16]

The significance of this argument for the current theological situation cannot be overestimated, for it explicitly maps the progressive decline of Christology through the consistent application of rationalistic Biblical criticism. For over a century, orthodox Christians have vainly reminded their liberal confréres of the Reformers' conviction that the "material principle" (the Gospel of Christ) cannot possibly survive apart from the "formal principle" (divinely inspired Scripture). "Fiddlesticks!" has been the reply: "*Of course* we can distinguish the true theological core of Scripture and the central message of Jesus from the Biblical thought-forms of the ancient Near East." But in point of fact, as Hamilton well shows, the stripping of the cultural thought-forms from the "true" teaching of Scripture is like peeling an onion: when finished, no substance remains.

Either Jesus' total teachings are taken as God's Word (including His full trust in Scripture as divine revelation) or, as Luther well put it, "everyone makes a hole in it wherever it pleases him, and follows his own opinions, interpreting and twisting Scripture any way he pleases." This is the inevitable outcome of a criticism that refuses to distinguish between straightforward grammatico-historical explication of the Biblical message and presuppositional judgment upon it.

The path to solid ground is the doctrine of total Biblical authority as taught by Christ Himself, at once the Lord of Scripture and its central figure.

If Christ did in fact "show himself alive after his passion by many infallible proofs" (Acts 1:3), thereby validating His claims to deity as He had predicted He would (Matthew 12:38-42; John 2:18-22), how can the Christian possibly rationalize a view of Scripture inconsistent with that of the Lord Christ? It will not do to argue in terms of modern "kenotic theory" that Jesus was limited or limited Himself to the thought-forms of His day, for (as Hamilton has well demonstrated) such hypothetical limitations have no boundaries and are logically capable of reducing everything Jesus said to meaninglessness. Moreover, as Eugene R. Fairweather concludes, after examining the whole kenotic question in detail: "It can hardly be claimed that Kenoticism is explicitly contained in the New Testament picture of Christ; rather, it depends on a complicated deduction, involving highly debatable presuppositions. . . . The Kenotic theory does not in fact vindicate the religious meaning of the Christian Gospel. On the contrary, in the severe words of Pius XII, it 'turns the integral mystery of the Incarnation and of redemption into bloodless and empty spectres.' " [17]

Nor does one accomplish anything by endeavoring to maintain that Jesus stamped with approval only the "substance" or "message" of the Bible, not its "form" or "medium," (on the assumption that only the message is important while the means of communication is inconsequential). As contemporary communications specialist Marshall McLuhan has shown in his epochal works,[18] the medium *is* the message." It is impossible to separate a message from its medium, since the medium makes an integral contribution to the very nature of the message. Orthodox Christianity has always recognized this in respect to Scripture: no "detail" of the Bible is unimportant; the literary form must itself be inspired in order for it not to detract from the message conveyed. Every word of Scripture — every "jot and tittle" of the text — has an impact, however slight, on the totality of the Bible, and this impact must, if Christ spoke truly, be for good.

How pertinent and intensely practical this issue of Biblical authority is for the theology and personal Christian testimony of believers today was brought out recently by Donald R. Neiswender, now a missionary in Japan. His "pilgrimage to faith in the integrity of Scripture" is recorded in *Christianity Today*, November 25, 1966; it warrants extended quotation here:

> From personal experience I well understand the theological attraction of an inspired yet errant Bible. Some years ago, while studying at a seminary in the Black Forest of Germany, I sat under two men who had taken their degrees under Karl Barth at the University of Basel. I had largely neglected Barth in my previous studies, and what a thrill it was to revel in the big, white volumes of *Die Kirchliche Dogmatik!* In what he said about Christ, how Barth nourished my soul! But though he often spoke highly of the Bible, Barth convinced me that there were errors, inaccuracies, and contradictions in the text. For the first time in my Christian life, I was faced with having to decide which verses of the Bible were authoritative for me and which were not.
>
> I clearly remember the morning when in my devotional time I read the first chapter of Hebrews, where the writer addresses to Jesus the verse from Psalm 45, "Thy throne, O God, is for ever and ever . . ." The thought came to me: How do I know that we ought to call Jesus *God?* Wasn't Hebrews written by an unknown author? And don't many theologians doubt whether it should be in the Bible?
>
> With deep shock I suddenly realized that, because I had come to limit the authority of the Bible, I no longer had any way to decide which verses were true. I had begun by believing that some records in the book of Kings contradict the books of Chronicles. I had gone on to wonder whether the Red Sea actually parted during the Exodus. I had doubted that Jonah could have lived for three days inside a fish. Now I was doubting whether or not Jesus was God.

For three days I struggled as the Christian Church struggled when it had to choose between the teachings of Arius and Athanasius. Like the Church, I chose to hold to faith in the full deity of Christ. And also like the Church, I made the decision because that is what the Bible teaches. Since that day the matter has been settled for me: To stick with the Bible is to stick with Christ. An inspired but errant Bible cannot teach me anything for certain, even about Christ. It cannot provide what I need more than life itself — assurance that my sins are forgiven.[19]

"More than life itself," modern secularized theology most certainly needs the assurance of the forgiveness of sins, and that assurance is available only through a totally trustworthy Biblical revelation. The relevance of Holy Scripture in the current theological bewilderment could hardly be more evident: only the Word of God, which stands forever, can offer solid footing for theologians needing to recover not only a saving Christ but also His God and Father.

THE RELEVANCE OF SCRIPTURE IN A DISENCHANTED ERA

The stir produced by the death-of-God movement is a genuine reflection of the loss of God by vast numbers of people in the twentieth century. In Samuel Beckett's play, *Waiting for Godot*, the leading characters are typical of modern man, waiting in darkness and addressing himself to the unknown god who never appears. At one point Vladimir says:

We wait. We are bored. (He throws up his hand.) No, don't protest, we are bored to death, there's no denying it. Good. A diversion comes along and what do we do? We let it go to waste. Come, let's get to work! (He advances towards the heap, stops in his stride.) In an instant all will vanish and we'll be alone once more, in the midst of nothingness.

Elsewhere in the play, Estragon remarks:

Yes, now I remember, yesterday evening we spent blathering about nothing in particular. That's been going on now half a century.[20]

How has such a cultural malaise come about in our time? Someone has sagely noted that in the eighteenth century the Bible died, in the nineteenth century God died, and in the twentieth century mankind has died. This sequence is not accidental: the rationalistic criticism of Scripture during the eighteenth century deistic "Enlightenment" removed the most solid foundation for belief in God; and after Nietzsche and other nineteenth-century thinkers proclaimed His demise, it became impossible any longer to substantiate man's individual worth. No longer a creature of God, man could only regard himself as a clever, evolving animal, and the totalitarianisms of the twentieth century are the inevitable result of stronger animals subjugating the weaker to their own ends. Without an eternal value system, available only in a veracious revelation from God, man is at the mercy of his fellows. Might makes right; in the words of Lord Acton's classic aphorism: "Power tends to corrupt; absolute power corrupts absolutely." Orwell's *1984* takes on nightmarish reality.

In the "secular theologians," however, an optimistic note is presently being sounded. A common axiom of the day, expressed by Cox and Altizer, is that "God is where the action is": in the dynamic social movements of our day, in the struggles for racial justice and human freedom. They assert that the "fully hidden Jesus" is now immanently to be experienced in such movements, and that "a whole new era in theology" is opening up through stress on the Spirit — "the God of the present."[21]

But what is the actual situation? Much of the social action of our day is indeed God-honoring, for all races are "one in Christ Jesus" (Galatians 3:28) and "God is no respecter of persons" (Romans 2:11, etc.); but apart from a revelatory, absolute ethic supra-cultural standards of justice cannot be established. This means that the "secular theologian" without an authoritative Scripture can as easily find himself embroiled in the demonic, racistic, fascist activism of a Third Reich as in the contemporary freedom marches in behalf of minorities. Only a firm Word of God, coming from outside the flux of contemporary action, can serve as a road map to an honorable and just future. And as the Reformers properly observed, talk about "Christ" or the "Spirit" apart from an objective Word is a waste of breath; for without a stable criterion, each man can build a demonic Christ — an antichrist — in his own image, and deceive many. The spirits, most definitely including the spirits of the age, must be tested

(I John 4:1); and the only touchstone remains the inscripturated Word.

The instability of current "action" philosophies and theologies is becoming evident as our contemporaries, à la Aldous Huxley and Timothy Leary, simultaneously seek answers in Eastern mysticism and reality-avoiding psychedelic drugs. Unconsciously, modern man recognizes that, whether in the metropolis or in the wilderness, whether in action or in silence, his heart, to recall Augustine's great truth, is restless till it rests in God. But to rest there, it must know who God is and what He has done for sinful man, and that can only be learned in the pages of Holy Writ.

Like the little lost creatures in Kenneth Grahame's *Wind in the Willows,* we long, each one of us, for "the piper at the Gates of Dawn."[22] How desperately we need to hear the clear piping of eternity as century twenty-one approaches! Well did a great theologian over a hundred years ago point disenchanted modern man to that clear voice of God recorded in the most relevant Book of all:

> Who can tell us whether this awful and mysterious silence, in which the Infinite One has wrapped himself, portends mercy or wrath? Who can say to the troubled conscience, whether He, whose laws in nature are inflexible and remorseless, will pardon sin? Who can answer the anxious inquiry whether the dying live on or whether they cease to be? Is there a future state? And if so, what is the nature of that untried condition of being? If there be immortal happiness, how can I attain it? If there be an everlasting woe, how can it be escaped? Let the reader close his Bible and ask himself seriously what he knows upon these momentous questions apart from its teachings. What solid foundation has he to rest upon in regard to matters, which so absolutely transcend all earthly experience, and are so entirely out of the reach of our unassisted faculties? A man of facile faith may perhaps delude himself into the belief of what he wishes to believe. He may thus take upon trust God's unlimited mercy, his ready forgiveness of transgressors, and eternal happiness after death. But this is all a dream. He knows nothing, he can know nothing about it, except by direct revelation from heaven.
>
> The question, therefore, is one of life or death. We will not, we can not give up our faith in the Bible. To do so is to surrender ourselves to blank despair. It is to blot out

the sun from the heavens and extinguish at once the very
source of light and life and holiness. "All flesh is as grass,
and all the glory of man as the flower of grass. The grass
withereth and the flower thereof falleth away; but the
WORD OF THE LORD endureth forever."[23]

He who has ears to hear the piping, let him hear!

Notes and Bibliography

Notes and Bibliography

For the convenience of the reader, footnotes and suggested bibliography as supplied by the several authors have been massed at the end of the Symposium. The listed titles are intended to aid those who desire to investigate more fully the subject matter contained in the individual essays. In some instances the footnotes will supply the references to broader bibliography.

I. THE MEANING OF THE WORD

1. *Phaedo* 85 D. See *Great Dialogues of Plato.* Translated by W. H. D. Rouse. Edited by Eric H. Warmington and Philip G. Rouse. (New York: New American Library of World Literature, 1956).

Bibliography:

Ockenga, Harold J., "The Glory of the Word of God" in *The Word of God and the Reformed Faith* (Grand Rapids, Mich.: Baker's Book Store, 1943). A statement of the Reformed position.

Reid, J. K. S., "The Theology of the Word" in *The Authority of Scripture* (New York: Harper & Brothers, n.d.), see pp. 194-233. A statement of the Neo-Orthodox position.

Runia, Klaas, *Karl Barth's Doctrine of Holy Scripture* (Grand Rapids, Mich.: Wm. B. Eerdmans Publishing Company, 1962). A thorough and fair critique of the Barthian Bibliology.

II. THE NECESSITY OF THE REVEALED WORD

1. See William Temple, *Nature, Man and God* (London, 1934, Lecture xii), and his essay in *Revelation,* ed. D. M. Baillie and H. Martin (London, 1937). For a critique, see J. I. Packer, *God Speaks to Man* (Philadelphia: Westminster Press, 1966), pp. 52 ff.

2. *Fundamentalism and the Word of God* (London and Grand Rapids: Eerdmans, 1958); *God Speaks to Man* (Philadelphia: Westminster Press, 1966: published in London, 1965, as *God Has Spoken*).

3. See for Reformed theology, H. Heppe, *Reformed Dogmatics* (E. T., London, 1950), p. 31 f.; for Lutheran theology, R. Preus, *The Inspiration of Scripture* (Edinburgh, 1955), pp. 23 ff.

4. *The Inspiration and Authority of Holy Scripture* (Philadelphia: Westminster Press, 1948), p. 219f.: from an article written in 1893. The last sentence is cited from an address of Warfield's own, published in 1880.

5. *Op. cit.,* p. 212.
6. L. Köhler, *Old Testament Theology* (Philadelphia: Westminster Press, 1957), p. 106.
Bibliography:
Kuyper, A., *Principles of Sacred Theology,* (Grand Rapids: Eerdmans, 1954).
Ramm, B. *Special Revelation and the Word of God,* (Grand Rapids: Eerdmans, 1961).
Works by Warfield and Calvin, as cited.

III. THE COMMUNICATION OF REVELATION

1. *Cf.* John Warwick Montgomery, *The "Is God Dead?" Controversy* (Grand Rapids: Zondervan, c. 1966). The proponents of this movement are not atheists; but they reject the traditional revelation of God and are seeking and, perhaps, expecting new concepts of God to come to light.
2. "Revelation," in John Baillie and Hugh Martin, eds., *Revelation* (New York: Macmillan, 1937), p. 83.
3. This is the view generally ascribed to Fundamentalists. Whether such an identification is valid depends entirely upon how one defines "Fundamentalist." If a Fundamentalist is defined as one who believes in a dictated Bible, such an identification of this view with Fundamentalism is logical enough. But, then, who calls himself a Fundamentalist in this sense? If Fundamentalism is Protestant orthodoxy of the late nineteenth and twentieth centuries, then it is difficult to find a Fundamentalist who has written in defense of such a view of revelation.
4. John Baillie summarizes brilliantly objections to this traditional viewpoint in his volume, *The Idea of Revelation in Recent Thought* (New York: Columbia University Press, 1956), p. 29.
5. See, for example, Karl Barth, *Das Christliche Verstaendnis der Offenbarung* (Munich: C. Kaiser Verlag, 1948), p. 3.
6. See, for example, Emil Brunner, *The Christian Doctrine of God* (trans. Olive Wyon. London: Lutterworth Press, 1949), p. 26.
7. Baillie, *op. cit.,* p. 29.
8. Albrecht Oepke, "Kalupto" in Gerhard Kittel, ed., *Theologisches Woerterbuch Zum Neuen Testamentum* (Stuttgart: W. Kohlhammer Verlag, 1938), Vol. III, *in loco.*
9. Baillie, *op. cit.,* p. 50.
10. *Ibid.* See also Paul Tillich, "Authority and Revelation," *Bulletin of Harvard Divinity School, Issue containing the Annual Lectures and Book Reviews for the Year, 1951-1952,* XLIX (April 7, 1952), p. 27; and William Temple, *Nature, Man and God* (London: Macmillan and Co. Ltd., 1960), p. 317.
11. Baillie, *op. cit.,* pp. 104-105.
12. *Eyes of Faith: A Study in the Biblical Point of View* (Philadelphia: The Westminster Press, 1946), p. 143.
13. Excerpt from his new book, *Heil als Geschichte,* soon to be published by Harper and Row. Professor Cullman's work has been translated by Sidney Sowers, Department of Religion, University of Tulsa, and this citation is used by permission.
14. Vincent Taylor, "Religious Certainty," *The Expository Times,* LXXII (November, 1960), pp. 49-52.
15. *The Bible Today* (New York: Macmillan, 1947), p. 351.
16. Oepke, *loc. cit.* (see above, *fn.* 8).
17. A *Greek-English Lexicon of the New Testament and Other Early Christian Literature* (tr. William F. Arndt and F. Wilbur Gingrich. 4th Ed., Chicago: Uni-

versity of Chicago Press, 1952), *in loco*. Bauer makes no claim that his list is complete.

18. For an extended treatment of other words for revelation, see Hannelis Schulte, *Der Begriff der Offenbarung im Neuen Testamentum* (Munich: C. Kaiser Verlag, 1949).

19. James Barr, "The Interpretation of Scripture," Part II — "Revelation through History in the Old Testament and in Modern Theology, Inaugural Address at Princeton Theological Seminary in December, 1962," *Interpretation*, Vol. XVII, No. 2 (April, 1963), pp. 201-202.

20. In recent years Calvin's teaching regarding a natural revelation has become the subject of heated theological dispute. See Brunner versus Barth [Emil Brunner and Karl Barth, *Natural Theology, Comprising "Nature and Grace" by Professor Emil Brunner and the Reply "No!" by Dr. Karl Barth* (trans. Peter Frankel. London: The Centenary Press, 1946)], and their respective seconds, Günter Gloede, *Theologia Naturalis bei Calvin* (Stuttgart: W. Kohlhammer, 1935); and Peter Barth, *Das Problem der Naturlichen Theologie bei Calvin, Theologische Existenz Heute* (eds. Karl Barth and Ed Thurneysen. München: Christian Kaiser, 1935). Note, however, the following: "Both heaven and earth contain innumerable proofs" — John Calvin, *Institutes of the Christian Religion* (trans. John Allen. Philadelphia: Presbyterian Board of Publications, 1813), I, 58; Calvin also writes: The order of the universe furnishes full "proof of the existence and perfection of God" — *Commentary on the Book of Psalms* (trans. James Anderson. Edinburgh: Calvin Translation Society, 1852-53), Vol. II, p. 310; in another passage Calvin notes that Nature is intended to "serve to bring us unto God" — *Sermons of Master John Calvin upon the Book of Job* (trans. Arthur Golding. London: Lucas Harrison and George Byshop, 1574), p. 159. In spite of the sufficiency of the data of natural revelation, however, Calvin warns that unregenerate man can never on this basis arrive at a knowledge of God. *Psalms*, II, 235; *Institutes*, I, 86; II, 261; *et passim*.

21. Julius Koestlin, *The Theology of Luther in Its Historical Development and Inner Harmony* (trans. Charles E. Hay. Philadelphia: Lutheran Publishing Society, c. 1897), pp. 18-20.

22. See Heinrich Heppe, *Reformed Dogmatics*, (rev. and ed. by Ernest Bizer, trans. G. T. Thompson. London: George Allen and Unwin, c. 1950), pp. 4 ff. and Heinrich Schmidt, *The Doctrinal Theology of the Evangelical Lutheran Church* (3rd ed., trans. Charles A. Hay and Henry E. Jacobs. Minneapolis: Augsburg, c. 1899), pp. 37-38.

23. L. Harold DeWolf, *The Religious Revolt Against Reason* (New York: Harper and Brothers, 1949).

24. *Nein, Passim.*

25. *Revelation and Reason: The Christian Doctrine of Faith and Knowledge* (Trans. Olive Wyon. Philadelphia: Westminster Press, c. 1946), p. 65.

26. *Institutes*, I, pp. 83, 84 and 87.

27. See Benjamin B. Warfield, "The Biblical Idea of Revelation," in *The Inspiration and Authority of the Bible* (Philadelphia: The Presbyterian Reformed Publishing Co., 1948), pp. 72 ff.

28. For some fine remarks concerning the adequacy of natural revelation and at the same time its radical inadequacy, see Cornelius Van Til, *Junior Systematics* (privately mimeographed syllabus, 1945), pp. 42 ff.

29. See George Ernest Wright and Reginald Fuller, *The God Who Acts* (Allenson Press: Naperville, Ill., 1957).

30. Note Deut. 13, Deut. 18, and John 20:30 and 31.

31. The precise psychological mediums of revelation are never clearly explained in

Biblical material. See Robert L. Alden, "Ecstasy and the Prophets," *Bulletin of the Evangelical Theological Society,* Vol. 9, No. 3, 1966, pp. 149-156; and C. H. Dodd, *The Authority of the Bible* (London: Fontana Press, 1960), pp. 61 ff. and Warfield, *Inspiration and Authority,* pp. 83 ff.

32. The Book of the Kings of Judah and Israel (This cannot be the canonical Book of Kings, for events mentioned are not all recorded there. I Chron. 26:11; 25:26; and 28:26); History of Samuel, the Seer (I Chron. 29:29); History of Nathan the Prophet (I Chron. 29:29); History of Gad, The Seer (I Chron. 29:29); Prophecy of Ahijah, the Shilonite (II Chron. 9:29); Vision of Iddo, the Seer (II Chron. 9:29); Histories of Shemaiah, the Prophet, and Iddo, the Seer (II Chron. 12:15); History of Jehu, the Son of Hanani (II Chron. 20:34); Commentary of the Book of the Kings (II Chron. 24:27); Acts of Uzziah by Isaiah, the Prophet, the Son of Amoz (II Chron. 26:22); Vision of Isaiah, the Prophet, the Son of Amoz (this could be our book of Isaiah, or only Isaiah 6; II Chron. 32:32); the Words of the Seers (or Hozai[?] II Chron. 33:19).

33. I Kings 11:41.

34. I Kings 14:29 and elsewhere.

35. I Kings 14:19 and elsewhere.

36. Even Karl Barth rebukes the theologians who presume to "look over their [Biblical authors'] shoulders benevolently or crossly to correct their notebooks." Rather, "Theology must agree to let them look over its 'shoulder' and correct its notebooks." *Evangelical Theology: An Introduction* (trans. Grover Foley. New York: Holt, Rinehart, and Winston, c. 1963), pp. 31-32.

37. Baillie, following many modern writers, includes illumination within the framework of revelation and does not clearly distinguish it from inspiration. *The Idea of Revelation,* pp. 64-66.

38. Note, for example, how in his discussion of illumination, Heppe relegates it to a later section of systematic theology and does not even discuss it under the heading of Scripture (*Reformed Dogmatics,* p. 80). Later evangelicals frequently buried the topic under the heading of the "Means of Grace," but fail to include a reference to it under the heading of Holy Scripture.

IV. THE PROBLEM OF COMMUNICATION

1. Acknowledgment is given to Dr. Francis A. Schaeffer, a missionary of L'Abri Fellowship, Switzerland, for much of the above material which he presented in lectures at Covenant Theological Seminary in 1965.

2. Benjamin B. Warfield, *The Inspiration and Authority of the Bible* (Philadelphia: Presbyterian and Reformed, [reprint of *Revelation and Inspiration*] 1948), p. 173.

3. Westminster Confession of Faith, I, 7.

4. R. Laird Harris, *Inspiration and Canonicity of the Bible* (Grand Rapids: Zondervan, 1957), pp. 28 ff., 104-128.

5. C. S. Lewis, *Miracles, A Preliminary Study* (New York: Macmillan, 1947).

6. R. Laird Harris, "Psalms" in *The Biblical Expositor,* ed. Carl F. H. Henry (Philadelphia: Holman, 1960), Vol. II, pp. 53-70.

7. For other such verses see the author's *Inspiration and Canonicity of the Bible,* pp. 57-66; J. Oliver Buswell, Jr., *A Systematic Theology of the Christian Religion* (Grand Rapids: Zondervan, 1962), Vol. I, pp. 198-212; also L. Gaussen, *The Inspiration of the Holy Scriptures* (Chicago: Moody Press [reprint] 1949), pp. 89-105.

8. Benjamin B. Warfield, *An Introduction to the Textual Criticism of the New Testament* (New York: Whittaker, 1889), p. 10.

V. Are the Scriptures Inerrant?

1. This relationship is, of course, denied. It should be noted, however, that this privative force is quite prevalent in English. When closing an unaccented syllable, the final "n" often assimilates and the following consonant is doubled, precisely as in Hebrew. Thus, for example, in-reparable becomes irreparable. In Spanish, however, this phenomenon does not always occur, *cf., inmediatamente*. Interesting examples of the privative force of the preposition are found in Babylonian.

2. I have sought to develop this point in *Thy Word Is Truth* (Grand Rapids: Eerdmans, 1964), pp. 113 ff.

3. Dewey M. Beegle, *The Inspiration of Scripture* (Philadelphia: The Westminster Press, 1963). We deeply appreciate the sincerity of this author and the courtesy which he manifests toward those of differing viewpoint. We do not feel, however, that the basic position espoused in this work is tenable, for it cannot be supported by Scripture.

4. *Op. cit.,* p. 66.

5. *Cf. e.g.,* the discussion in Alan Richardson: *History Sacred and Profane* (Philadelphia: Westminster Press, 1964), pp. 213 ff.

6. Bruce Vawter: *A Pathway Through Genesis* (New York: Sheed & Ward, [1956]), p. 48.

7. The characteristics of Hebrew poetry are lacking in Genesis One. *Cf.* my *Studies in Genesis One* (Philadelphia: Presbyterian and Reformed Publishing Company, 1964), pp. 82-86.

8. *Cf. e.g.,* J. L. MacKenzie: "Myth and the Old Testament," in *The Catholic Biblical Quarterly,* Vol. XXI, July, 1959, p. 281.

9. I have sought to develop this point in *Studies in Genesis One,* pp. 15ff., 87ff.

10. It is, of course, unnecessary to speak of ultimate origin, for the word "origin" itself contains such a reference. Nevertheless, inasmuch as so many speak of the origin of the earth, etc., and by such language have in mind merely the formation of the earth and heavenly bodies from pre-existing materials, it seems best to employ the adjective "ultimate" in order to make clear that the reference is to the creation of earth.

11. *Cf.* Young, *op. cit.,* pp. 93ff., and Karlheinz Rabast, *Die Genesis,* Berlin, 1951, p. 48.

12. The Hebrew word מִין (min.) is not a precise equivalent of English "species." It is a general term with fairly broad connotation.

13. *Cf.* B. B. Warfield, "On the Antiquity and Unity of the Human Race," *Princeton Theological Review,* 1911.

14. We hold, for reasons stated elsewhere, that in its present form, Genesis is essentially the work of Moses, and it is the Mosaic age to which we have reference in the text. That in the compilation of Genesis Moses may have employed previously existing documents is quite likely, and if this was the case, it would to some extent explain some of the phenomena which the negative critics seek to explain as due to the presence of later, post-Mosaic documents.

15. For an interesting recent presentation of this material, *cf.* S. G. F. Brandon, *Creation Legends of the Ancient Near East* (London: Hodder and Stoughton, 1963).

16. G. von Rad: *Genesis* (The Old Testament Library), tr. by John H. Marks (Philadelphia: Westminster Press, 1961), holds that chapter one is priestly doctrine, which has been carefully enriched over the centuries by very slow growth ("—es ist Lehre, die im langsamstem, jahrhundertelangem Wachstum sich behutsam angereichert hat.").

17. Beegle, *op. cit.,* has listed a number of the more serious difficulties.

18. For the presentation of a Christian-Biblical apologetic *cf.* Cornelius Van Til, *The Defense of the Faith* (Philadelphia: Presbyterian and Reformed Publishing Company, 1963).

19. *Cf. Thy Word Is Truth,* pp. 261ff.

20. As an introduction to the subject, *cf.* Edwin R. Thiele: *The Mysterious Numbers of the Hebrew Kings* (Chicago: University of Chicago Press, 1951), Revised Edition (Grand Rapids, Mich.: Wm. B. Eerdmans Publishing Company, 1965).

21. *Cf.* Robert Dick Wilson, *Studies in the Book of Daniel* (New York: G. P. Putnam's Sons, 1917), pp. 43-59; E. J. Young, *The Prophecy of Daniel* (Grand Rapids: Wm. B. Eerdmans Publishing Company, 1953), pp. 267-270.

22. *Cf.* H. H. Rowley: "Hezekiah's Reform and Rebellion," in *Bulletin of the John Rylands Library,* Vol. 44, No. 2. In *The Prophecy of Isaiah,* Vol. II, (Eerdmans), I propose to discuss this question in detail.

23. This position was given classic expression by S. R. Driver, *An Introduction to the Literature of the Old Testament* (Edinburgh: T. & T. Clark, 1913), p. 508.

24. *Cf.* O. T. Allis, *The Five Books of Moses* (Philadelphia: Presbyterian and Reformed Publishing Company, 1943).

25. Ephraim A. Speiser, *Genesis* (The Anchor Bible; New York: Doubleday, 1964), p. 5.

26. *Cf. Studies in Genesis One,* pp. 73-76.

27. Tr. by R. B. Bjornard, New York, 1959, p. 14.

28. *Cf.* Hayim Tadmor, "The Campaigns of Sargon II of Assur: A Chronological-Historical Study," in *Journal of Cuneiform Studies,* Vol. XII, pp. 22-40, 77-100.

VI. The Inspiration of the Old Testament

1. B. B. Warfield, *The Inspiration and Authority of the Bible* (Philadelphia: Presbyterian & Reformed Publishing Company, 1948), p. 131.

2. *Ibid.*

3. James Barr, *Semantics of Biblical Language* (London: Oxford University Press, 1961), pp. 129-140.

4. Th. C. Vriezen, *An Outline of Old Testament Theology,* Translated by S. Nenijen (Wageningen: H. Veenman, 1958), p. 95.

5. *Op. cit.,* p. 229.

VII. The Inspiration of the New Testament

1. See Protestant Donald Evans, "Protestant and Roman Views of Revelation," *Canadian Journal of Theology,* 10 (1964) 258-65, and the reply by Catholic J. Martucci, *ibid,* 265-270.

2. See especially K. Runia, *Karl Barth's Doctrine of Holy Scripture* (Grand Rapids: Eerdmans, 1962).

3. J. Murray, *The Infallible Word* (Grand Rapids, Mich.: Eerdmans, 1946), p. 33.

4. See K. H. Rengstorf, "Apostolos," *Theological Dictionary of the N.T.,* I, 407-445; N. Geldenhuys, *Supreme Authority* (London: Marshall, Morgan, Scott, 1953).

Bibliography:

Geldenhuys, N., *Supreme Authority* (London: Marshall, Morgan, Scott, 1953).

Stonehouse, N. B., "The Authority of the New Testament," *The Infallible Word,* (Grand Rapids: Eerdmans, 1946).

Ridderbos, H. N., *The Authority of the New Testament Scriptures* (Philadelphia: Presbyterian and Reformed Publishing Co., 1963).

Ramm, B., *Special Revelation and the Word of God* (Grand Rapids: Eerdmans, 1961).

VIII. THE MESSAGE OF THE WORD

IX. THE PRAGMATIC CONFIRMATION OF SCRIPTURAL AUTHORITY

1. David W. Kerr, "Augustine of Hippo," in *Inspiration and Interpretation,* Ed. John F. Walvoord (Grand Rapids, Michigan: William B. Eerdmans Publishing Company, 1957), pp. 74-75.
2. Loraine Boettner, *The Inspiration of the Scriptures* (Grand Rapids, Michigan: William B. Eerdmans Publishing Company, 1937), p. 65.
3. R. B. Kuyper, *The Infallible Word: A Symposium* (Philadelphia: The Presbyterian Guardian Publishing Corporation, 1946), pp. 253-54.

X. THE RELEVANCE OF SCRIPTURE TODAY

1. Quotation in "Church for Unbelievers" in *Newsweek,* XLV (April 26, 1965), p. 62.
2. Reinhold Niebuhr, "The Unity of History," *Christianity and Crisis,* II (May 4, 1942), 1.
3. See Philip E. Hughes, Ed., *Introduction to Dogmatic Theology,* by Edward Arthur Litton (London: J. Clarke, [1960]), p. 19.
4. Justus, Hartnack, *Wittgenstein and Modern Philosophy.* Translated by Maurice Cranston (New York: New York University Press, 1956), p. ix.
5. Ludwig Wittgenstein, *Tractatus Logico-Philosophicus* (London: Harcourt, 1922). See 6.41-6.421.
6. John W. Montgomery, "Where Is History Going?" *Religion In Life,* 33 (2, Spring, 1964), 238-255.
7. Arthur C. Danto, *Analytical Philosophy of History* (Cambridge: Cambridge University Press, 1965), pp. 12-13.
8. G. E. Moore, *Principia Ethica* (Cambridge: University Press, 1922). See Chapter 1.
9. Kurt Baier, *The Moral Point of View* (New York: Random House, 1965), p. 157.
10. Ludwig Wittgenstein, "A Lecture on Ethics," in *Philosophical Review,* LXXIV (January, 1965), 3-11.
11. *Cf.* Wittgenstein's *Lectures and Conversations on Aesthetics, Psychology, and Religious Belief,* Ed. Cyril Barrett (Oxford: Blackwell, 1966), pp. 57-59.
12. Norman Malcom, *Ludwig Wittgenstein, A Memoir* (London: Oxford University Press, 1958), p. 32: "He was constantly depressed, I think, by the impossibility of arriving at understanding in philosophy."
13. J. W. N. Watkins in *La Philosophie au milieu du vingtième siècle,* Ed. R. Klibansky. Second Edition. (Firenze: 1961-1962). Vol. III, p. 159.
14. Elder Olson, "Hamlet and the Hermeneutics of Drama," in *Modern Philology* 61 (1962-63), pp. 235-237.
15. Paul Edwards, "Professor Tillich's Confusions," *Mind,* LXXIV (April, 1965), pp. 195-214.
16. *The Death of God Debate,* Edd. J. L. Ice and J. J. Carey (Philadelphia: Westminster Press, 1967), pp. 222, 223.
17. F. W. Beare, *A Commentary on the Epistle to the Philippians* (New York: Harper & Bros., Publishers, [1959]), p. 173.

18. Marshall McLuhan, *The Gutenberg Galaxy* (Toronto: The University of Toronto Press, 1962).
19. Donald R. Neiswander, "Found Too Late: The Word of God," in *Christianity Today*, XI (November 25, 1966), 7, 8.
20. Samuel Beckett, "Waiting for Godot" in *Seven Plays for the Modern Theater* (New York: Grove Press, 1962).
21. "Stress on the Spirit" in *Time* 88 (August 5, 1966), p. 69.
22. Kenneth Grahame, *The Wind in the Willows* (New York: The Heritage Press, pp. 92-103).
23. Wm. Henry Green, *The Pentateuch* (New York: J. Wiley, 1863).

Bibliography:

Henry, Carl F. H. (Ed.). *Jesus of Nazareth: Saviour and Lord* (Grand Rapids, Michigan: Eerdmans, 1966).

Lawrenz, Carl J. (Ed.). *This Steadfast Word: A Series of Essays on the Holy Scriptures* (Milwaukee, Wisconsin: Northwestern Publishing House, 1965).

Montgomery, John Warwick, *Crisis in Lutheran Theology.* 2 vols. (Grand Rapids, Michigan: Baker Book House, 1967).

Montgomery, John Warwick. *The 'Is God Dead?' Controversy* (Grand Rapids, Michigan: Zondervan, 1966).

Valen-Sendstad, Olav, *The Word That Can Never Die.* Translated by Madson and Strand (St. Louis, Missouri: Concordia Publishing House, 1966).